Minnesota Memories 4

by Joan Cla

Five million people now cal
mission to statehood nearly
80,000 square miles has give
the fertile river valleys and bluff country to the vast northwestern prairies
to the Boundary Waters Canoe Area, to Lake Superior's harbors, and the
diverse sophistication of metropolitan areas, Minnesota people have accepted the bounty and taken on the challenges.

I have lived on both the West and East Coast. Whenever I mentioned that
I was born in Minnesota, folks started talking slower. Their perception of
Minnesotans, based on characters in *The Golden Girls* and *Fargo*, is that
we are... Ole and Lena! Although I defensively pointed out Minnesota's
top ranking in lists of achievements and rattled off a litany of Minnesota
contributions to society, my diatribes failed to dispel these stereotypes.

I wondered why Minnesotans tolerated pop culture's negative portrayals.
Why should anyone from a state that produced the Mayo Clinic, Sinclair
Lewis, F. Scott Fitzgerald, three Rock 'n Roll Hall of Famers, world class
theaters and orchestras, Scotch Tape, two vice presidents, World Series
champs, the Pacemaker, the thermostat, water skis, Charles Schulz and
Charles Lindburgh accept disdain from the hayseed police?

Three years ago I decided it might be fun to travel around the state collecting true stories from real Minnesotans so that they might help set the record
straight. I figured I'd put *Minnesota Memories* volumes out there in stores
and libraries so that the world might get a chance to see what diverse,
honorable, smart, strong, capable, creative, witty, thoughtful and good-
humored people we really are. I've acquired many friends on my travels.

Minnesota Memories stories run the gamut--from tragic to hilarious to
heroic to merely reflective. The majority of contributors are ordinary people
making their contribution to recorded Minnesota history. Their stories are
extraordinary, and best of all--they're true. This is Minnesota history of
the people, by the people, and for the people. I hope these real Minnesota
stories help dispel those joke and fiction-based stereotypes, and I hope
you have as much fun reading as I had collecting them.

Joan Claire Graham, the Purveyor of Memories

Minnesota Memories 4
Table of Contents

Cover photo by Aquinata "Cookie" Graham. Thanks, Mom!
Back Cover photo by Leah Nell Peterson, Cannon Falls Beacon

ISBN: 0971 1971 3X

Minnesota Memories 4 Copyright 2004   Graham Megyeri Books,
439 Lakeview Blvd, Albert Lea, MN 56007   MinnMemory @aol.com
All Rights Reserved. No part of this book may be reprinted without
permission from the publisher.

76 Trombones and a Few Million Fish Flies
by Joan Claire Graham

When my daughters attended high school in the 1990s, they received recruitment materials from colleges and universities throughout the country. By senior year, we had hundreds of letters, videos, pamphlets, catalogs and brochures. Choosing their colleges involved studying promotional material, talking to experts, applying for scholarships, visiting campuses, interviewing representatives and alumni, and careful consideration.

Such was not the case when I chose to attend Winona State back in 1964. My parents did not have money to send me to a private college, so my three options were the University of Minnesota, Mankato State and Winona State. All three were located within 100 miles of my Albert Lea home, and all offered a bachelor's degree for the unbelievable bargain basement price of approximately $5 per quarter credit. A full quarter's tuition cost less than $100. What a deal.

According to my mother and father, it was an open and shut case. My grandmother lived in Mankato, my uncle and brother and cousins had attended "T.C.," and my fate was sealed. Mankato State College would be my choice. Their determination, along with feeling deprived of the freedom to choose from among my three measly options, tripped my adolescent rebellion buttons. I talked to a representative from Winona State at a college fair and signed up to be on their mailing list. I had driven through Winona once and admired the bluffs and scenic river setting.

A packet of Winona State material arrived a few days later. One flyer advertised a special summer program in which I could earn eight credits for five weeks' work on a summer theater production of *The Music Man*. That was it. I wanted to be in that musical. Not only was I going to attend Winona State, but I was starting college a week after high school graduation. Ignoring academic or social considerations, I made this critical life decision based on my desire for instant gratification. Without visiting the campus or talking to anybody who had attended the school, I chose Winona State so that I could sing and dance in *The Music Man* in July of 1964. I'm embarrassed to admit to being so shallow, but there you have it.

After a fair amount of yelling, my parents allowed me to have my way, and a week after graduation, after Sunday mass, we piled my stuff into the Ford and headed off to Winona. I don't think my parents had ever seen the town, and after we passed through Rochester and headed east on old highway 14, I started to have trepidations about going so far away from home so soon after graduation.

True to form, my dad got us on the road early, and we were the first to arrive at old Shepard Hall around 10 a.m. The college staff wasn't on duty yet, so we drove around town for awhile and grabbed a quick lunch at McVey's on Huff Street. The dorm opened at noon, and as my dad impatiently took my bags out of the car, somebody handed me keys, my roommate's name, a couple of sheets, a pillow case, a list of rules, and directions to the cafeteria, laundry room, and community bathroom.

Summer school lacked orientation and welcoming committees so I felt incredibly lonely after my parents left. Since I had never even attended summer camp, I felt the enormity of this abrupt transition from home to the big world, and after I unpacked my suitcases in the last room on the east side of the first floor, I lay down on the bare little bed and cried until I fell asleep. When I awoke, I got on my bicycle and rode all over town.

As the day wore on, Shepard and Morey Halls filled with students. The majority were older teachers returning for workshops and classes needed to complete certification or advanced degrees. I was the only dorm resident involved in the musical theater workshop.

Class registration the next day was chaotic and confusing. Boxes of cards sat on tables, and representatives from academic departments supervised the distribution, or "pulling" of cards. When all cards had been pulled, the class was filled. Registration involved standing in lines to receive advice, pull cards, fill out forms, and pay fees. There was no air conditioning, and temperatures were climbing.

After pulling my cards for Musical Theater Workshop, I found the rehearsal hall and met Richmond McClure and Jacques Reidelberger, co-directors and scene designer. Realizing they had a short time to pull the show together, they began work immediately.

I got the part of a dancing, singing River City teenager, which was great. The starring roles of Marian the librarian and Professor Harold Hill were double cast, so although my role was small, I was happy to be able to be needed in all four performances. Rehearsals began the first day. In the morning we learned songs, and in the afternoon we learned dances in old Somsen Auditorium. When we weren't rehearsing, we painted and built scenery, sewed costumes, sold tickets, and did whatever else was needed.

Female dancers outnumbered males, so the desperate choreographer went into the Smog and recruited a couple of guys who were sitting around eating burgers. Seduced by the opportunity to earn eight credits without taking any tests or even cracking open a book, a couple of business majors with no prior experience or interest in theater, dancing or music agreed to round out the group of eight River City dancing teenagers. One of these guys turned out to be my partner, and the best thing I can say about him is that he had two legs, didn't step on my feet too much, and was only a little bit shorter than me.

Winona is a river city so it was a great place to stage that show. College and civic organizers had pooled their talent and money to produce *The Music Man* as part of the town's annual Steamboat Days celebration. Thousands of people bought buttons that admitted them to several Steamboat Days events, including the final performance of *The Music Man*. The first three performances of the show would take place in Somsen Auditorium, where anybody could buy a ticket and watch the show. The final performance would take place out in the elements, come rain or shine, on the final night of Steamboat Days at Levee Park on the Mississippi River.

Rehearsals and preparations rolled along flawlessly for a few days until one morning when director Jacques Reidelberger came in with a concerned expression and a report from Dr. Calvin Fremling, biology professor and nationally recognized expert in the study of may flies. May flies, seasonal pests in river areas, spend the first two years of their life cycle among the fish in the river--unnoticed by humans. During their last 72 hours, they molt, turn into greasy dragonfly-like critters, mate, lay eggs, fly and die. Winona natives prefer to call them fish flies, and during the '60s, fish flies were at their reproductive peak in the Winona area.

Attracted by light, fish flies spend their final hours surrounding street lights and store signs, creating an incredible cloud and a flutter of sound and movement. In a few hours, they weaken and fall. By morning, most are dead, leaving millions of greasy gossamer bodies on roadways, bridges, porches, decks, sidewalks and ball fields. Baseball games in Winona were sometimes canceled because nobody could see the ball amidst clouds of fish flies. Traffic accidents occurred after greasy carcasses slickened roads, and snowplows were sometimes deployed to clean bug bodies from bridges. Store owners shoveled dead flies from their entryways and sidewalks. Fish flies, for a few hours every summer, became a plague.

According to Dr. Fremling's calculations, the next fish fly hatching was due to take place the night of the big performance of *The Music Man* at Levee Park. The first bright lights they would be attracted to would be those used to light the stage. With 5,000 Steamboat Days buttons sold, the hatching would undoubtedly gross out at least half that many audience members and most performers. A cloud of fish flies was starting to darken over this production of *The Music Man.*

The directors were somewhat encouraged by the possibility that if Dr. Fremling's calculations were off by just a couple of hours, the hatching might take place after and not during the performance. This was their only sliver of hope that their extravaganza would be saved from ruin, but the show must go on, so they forged ahead with rehearsals and production details. Dr. Fremling's prediction turned out to be only the first hint of several disasters that would eventually challenge *The Music Man.*

The weather also posed problems as a record-breaking heat and humidity spell set in. Temperatures climbed to the 90s and stayed there for the entire period of rehearsal and construction. Campus air conditioning was limited to the president's office, so those of us dancing in the auditorium, singing in the rehearsal room, rehearsing on stage, building scenery backstage, and trying to sleep in the dorm at night were forced to stew in our own juices. I peeled off my sodden clothes and took three showers every day, which produced heat-related consequences because the wrinkled casual look in clothing didn't exist. Every Saturday morning I washed and ironed twenty blouses--my entire summer supply.

Adjacent to my dorm room was the smoking lounge, where every day I purchased at least five bottles of Royal Crown Cola from a machine that managed to stay stocked. I hate to think of how hyper I must have been from all that sugar and caffeine, but at least I kept dehydration at bay.

As opening night approached, the show came together nicely, but we faced other problems. Advanced sales for the indoor performances were so brisk that the house manager, who had never experienced a sold out house with reserved seats, noticed that most of the stenciled numbers on the auditorium seats had been scratched off. He gave me an ink pad and one of those library date stampers and told me to stamp numbers on the backs of all the wooden seats. When I told him that the ink would run, he showed me a seat that he had experimented on, and its dried ink didn't rub off on his hand. I went around the auditorium and stamped numbers on all the seats that needed numbers--hundreds of them.

When Fred Heyer brought in his orchestra, cast members had to learn to project their voices because horns were so much louder than our rehearsal piano, and the auditorium had no microphones. Someone made a note to get microphones for the outdoor performance.

One of the Harold Hill actors was a Caledonia music teacher whose dark hair was thinning. As chairman of the makeup committee, I devised a solution I thought would make him look more like a leading man. On opening night, I sprayed his pate with dark colored hairspray, and from a distance he looked great. But as the heat soared, Professor Hill began a geyser- like sweat that caused the dark hairspray to drizzle down his face and produce a ghoulish Alice Cooper effect. When it came time to change costumes, Harold's streaked and saturated clothing had to be peeled from his body as fellow cast members ducked out of the way of the spray.

Despite all this, the show went well. Audience members packed the auditorium and nobody died of heatstroke. Stage lighting raised the heat even more, and it's fair to say that everyone in the audience and on the stage was soaked to the skin by the end of the first act. At the final chorus of "76 Trombones," audience members rose from their seats and caused a slight breeze with their clapping and cheering.

The next day I heard several theater-goers complain about black marks that wouldn't come off the backs of their shirts, and I noticed that all my carefully applied numbers had disappeared from the wooden seat backs.

After three successful indoor performances, we worked all day July 12 to transport scenery and lights six blocks and set them up at Levee Park for the final show. Someone rigged pipes for lights and a scaffold tower for the follow spot. Electricians ran cables while singers tested the three microphones on stands that someone had rigged up. We had a brief run through that included scenery shifts and sound tests. The sky was clear, thousands of spectator benches and seats had been set up, and no fish flies had hatched yet, but by late afternoon, a brisk wind was blowing upstage--away from the audience. It became obvious that it would be difficult for audience members to hear the miked actors and the unmiked orchestra.

As thousands of spectators took their seats in Levee Park, and river boats pulled up to watch and listen, the overture began, and the fish flies started hatching. As luck would have it, the gusting wind kept the insects off the actors and audience. Unfortunately that very same wind blew the sound waves away from the audience and the scenery away from the stage.

Jacques Reidelberger grabbed every actor who was not onstage and told them to grab a scenery piece, a microphone stand, or a curtain and hang on for dear life. If they had to leave their post to go onstage, they had to draft a substitute scenery holder. It was impossible to hide from the audience as gusts twisted scenery pieces this way and that. Some large pieces and all the curtains required several human anchors, without whose effort River City scenery would have ended up in Wabasha. I often wonder if that's where the sound waves went, because nobody in the audience could hear--despite three microphones on stands that kept blowing over.

 As the night became darker and wilder, and the "Pick a Little, Talk a Little" song wore on, I looked toward the spotlight tower, and behind a cloud of fish flies, I could see the terrified face of the light operator who hung on tightly as the wind blew his tower six feet forward with every gust. If any safety inspectors had still been sober after a weekend of Steamboat Days festivities, they would have certainly stopped the show.

By the middle of the first act, audience members started to bail out. They couldn't hear because of the wind, they couldn't see because of the fish flies, they were afraid of being hit by falling lights, and they had grown tired of watching actors hang on to scenery.

By the time the cast and orchestra played and sang the "76 Trombones" finale, crowd size had shrunk from two thousand to eight people. I suspect those eight were either people who needed rides home from cast members or theater historians who wanted to be there for the most disastrous performance of *The Music Man* ever produced in the American theater. The next day I heard lots of complaints about what a lousy show it had been, but I still feel that those critics were unduly harsh. When the forces of nature go up against art, nature almost always gets the upper hand.

We struck the set the following day and said goodbye to cast and crew. With my first summer session of college behind me, I settled in for the long haul that included a much more realistic set of academic expectations. The 4.0 average that I earned in Musical Theater Workshop was impossible to maintain in those days when the bell curve still existed, but I never regretted choosing Winona State. Although my college selection process had been based on shallow criteria, my first college experience had been memorable and had bonded me to the place. And all those disastrous aspects of *The Music Man* formed a baseline by which all future calamities could be measured.

Cast members of Winona State's 1964 production of The Music Man, taken before the set blew away in a cloud of fish flies. Ricky McCluer, Liz Gunhus, Mrs. Van Alstine, Bert Dibbley.

Return of an Expatriate Pack Rat
by Joan Claire Graham

After an 18-year absence, I moved back to Minnesota this year, to a 100 year-old house on the lake, just a couple of blocks from where I grew up in Albert Lea. It's great to be back in Minnesota, but moving was an incredible amount of work, and it's going to take a long time to recover.

As I sorted through things to pack I heard friends say, "If you haven't used it in a year, throw it out." For many people, this advice makes sense, but those of us who describe ourselves as pack rats need different criteria to discard treasures and trash from the past. My visual sense is deductive rather than inductive. I can not draw or invent in my imagination a visual image, but the sight of an image can trigger memories of events, names, emotions, places and stories, and I fear that if I toss the stuff that primes the pump, I'll lose those memories forevermore.

My daughter Susannah, who helped me sort through old clothes, was shocked when I refused to part with a few things she thought were absolutely worthless. She thought, for instance, that I should get rid of that maternity dress I haven't needed since she was born in 1979 and a Butte Knit suit my mother gave me her last Christmas before she died. How can I explain to someone who hasn't experienced either the birth of a child or the death of a parent how just seeing those things brings back a flood of memories that I can't bear to give up?

I have a trunk filled with little girls' clothes, and each item triggers a memory about one of my daughters--a birthday party, a piano recital, a school play, Halloween, Christmas celebrations and first days of school. These clothes might be appreciated by a stranger who pays a couple of bucks for them at the Goodwill, but how would I replace those memory boosters? The enjoyment I get from remembering those good times is well worth the space the trunk takes up.

When I was a child, my mother kept scrapbooks and photo albums, and I never tired of looking through them. She saved all the cards I received for special occasions, a lock of my curly baby hair, all my Iowa Basic

Skills Test results and report cards and some letters I received from friends and relatives when I was sick with rheumatic fever. When I got older, I made my own rock 'n roll scrapbook and a high school scrapbook. I made scrapbooks for my kids, but they haven't enjoyed looking at them as much as I enjoyed making them. Just because they haven't been used in a year, however, doesn't mean I should throw them out, even though my scrapbook collection fills two trunks.

When I graduated from junior high to high school, I took a sensible approach and saved only enough grade school stuff to fill a little red memory box. Those items, still in that plastic box, include the blue iron-on letters from my ninth grade cheerleader uniform--SM (St. Mary's, not Sado Masochism). I have a folder printed with the school name and some businesses that provided the folder, some class pictures and a color photo of a Halloween costume party Carol Bergen and I threw in her basement when we were in ninth grade, some birthday cards and notes from friends. There's a picture of me in a cotton-puckered swimsuit at the beach. I re-member buying that suit and matching cover-up at Spurgeons.

When I moved from high school to college, we easily loaded everything I needed into a car that already contained two parents, myself and my little sister. When I moved from my first teaching job I had to make two or three trips with my stuff loaded in a Ford Falcon. The next time I had to rent a small U-Haul. After I bought my piano, a move required a small moving van; then, as my empire expanded, I needed bigger and bigger trucks. My personal collection just keeps growing, but its actual value remains about the same as always. It's not worth much.

I still have my collection of 45 records. Need I explain their impor-tance? How many parties did I take them to? I had to babysit four hours at 25 cents an hour to buy one record.   How many times did I fall in love with Frankie Avalon while listening to "Venus?" I still have three or four volumes of Dick Clark's Greatest Hits. I sent Beechnut gum wrappers and money to get them, and they're still in their original jackets.

Some of my pack rat behavior is weird. For instance, I can't throw away old address books because they contain all that remains of former friends and relatives.

Some have died, others have drifted away and lost contact, but seeing their names triggers memories. I have a box that contains a dress my grandma crocheted, and when I open the box I can smell my grandma's house in Mankato. I have a cup that says "South Dakota Sis" my friend Carol Adair bought me when her family went to the Black Hills, and I treasure the Beatrix Potter and Holly Hobbie plastic dishes I ordered for my kids with Betty Crocker coupons.

Some of my junk relates to my teaching career. I ran across a folder of funny answers from tests. One question on a drama test was, "What are royalties, and why must we obey laws concerning them?"

A boy named Mike Fortin wrote, "Royalties are the director and producer of the play, and if you don't obey their rules, they'll throw you out of the show." I laugh every time I read that, and remember the little blond eighth grader who knew more about golf than he knew about theater. I have some slides from junior high plays I directed. I don't have a slide projector, but when I hold the slides up to the light I can remember names of cast members-- like Wendy Gutenkauf, Brian Junker, Ted Hanson and Cecile Burzynski. They must be in their 40s now, but I remember them as kids. If I toss out the slides I might forget them.

Before moving back to Minnesota, I managed to discard several car loads of furniture and clothes I didn't want anymore, and I threw out teaching materials because the originals are on disk. But the amount of stuff I packed into two Ryder trucks I drove from Maryland was staggering-- tons of books, lots of old clothes, my doll collection, my 45s, 33s, and 78 rpm records, my mother's set of seldom-used Bavarian China, the bedspread my grandmother crocheted, my grandmother's old steamer trunk, the outfit I bought for my twenty-first birthday, and a 1973 coat I've always liked. Neighbors in Maryland shook their heads, watched me load, and couldn't believe my mountain of junk.

When I arrived in Minnesota, I encountered a new breed of neighbor. Folks who didn't know me from a hole in the ground showed up at my door to help me unload. One neighbor got off her bike and pitched right in. The woman next door gave me lunch, and in the afternoon both she and her husband made several trips from the truck to my house with armloads of stuff. The fellow who lives on the other side joined in. My insurance guy stopped by, took off his suit coat and helped carry some heavy bookcases. They probably talked about my mountain of junk afterwards, but at the time I needed assistance they unselfishly gave their time and energy.

That willingness to help is something I missed when I lived in other places. I like to joke that I could have died unloading my junk in California and Maryland, and the neighbors would have stepped over my parched bones and complained about the smell.

But there are drawbacks about living in Minnesota. After nearly two decades in more moderate climates, I thought I had lost my ability to feel chilly. But when the temperature dropped to 18 below zero in January, I discovered otherwise. St. Paul Winter Carnival officials closed the Ice Palace because they didn't want their workers to freeze. You know it's cold when it's too cold to keep the Ice Palace open.

Despite winter's cold sting, it's good to be back in North Star State. The people are nice, the town has natural beauty and plenty of opportunities for civic involvement, and the cost of living is more comfortable for a small time writer and retiree. But beyond all that, I'm glad for one more thing. My big old house on the lake has lots of space for my mountains of memories.

Working for Room and Board
by Joan Claire Graham

I often go out of my way to drive past the place where my mother worked for her room and board, a beautiful stucco and brick Tudor revival three-story house--a mansion really--at 126 East Franklin in Minneapolis. Three chimneys suggest several fireplaces within, and dozens of windows hint at the presence of many rooms no longer considered important by today's architects--a music room, a parlor, a pantry, a sleeping porch and maybe a library. A portico and carriage house on an old photo she took provide a history lesson about how things used to be.

Now listed on the National Registry of Historic Places, this home was built in 1906 by architect Edwin Hewitt, who also designed the Hennepin Avenue Methodist Church, the Cathedral Church of St. Mark's, and other Minneapolis landmarks. A prominent architect deserved a distinguished home of his own, and Hewitt's house still stands as a testament to his art and skill.

The folks who built big houses near the turn of the last century needed servants to clean and maintain their property. I don't know if Hewitt's servants lived in the basement or in little rooms beneath third floor dormers. Either Mom didn't talk much about it, or I didn't listen.

The Edwin Hewitt House, 126 E. Franklin in Minneapolis

After graduating from Madison Lake's All Saints High School in 1929, Mom studied violin and drama at McPhail's Conservatory at 12th and LaSalle in Minneapolis. Like many young people those days, Mother didn't have any money and was expected to work for her room and board, so she signed on as a servant in that grand house on Franklin. It was a good thing she had such a formidable roof over her head and a couple of square meals each day because shortly after she began her studies, the stock market crashed and jobs became scarce.

Despite hard times during the Great Depression, people who owned those big houses had to maintain them, and bartering food and shelter for much-needed help seemed like a sensible thing for all concerned. The Hewitt house had windows to clean, floors to scrub, several fireplaces to sweep, woodwork and hearths to polish, bedrooms to maintain, a ballroom and chandeliers to polish and a pipe organ to dust. Mother rolled up her sleeves and worked many hours in the house each week, and walked or took the streetcar to nearby McPhail for her classes.

Young men and women who worked for their room and board had to be willing to abide by their employer's house rules and spend a reasonable amount of time pitching in to do whatever needed to be done back in the days before automatic washers and dryers, wash 'n wear fabrics, dishwashers and vacuum cleaners. Silverware and tea services needed to be polished, wet laundry needed to be hung on lines, and rugs had to be taken out and beaten. Maintaining those big houses required a lot of work.

Not all room and board situations were set in homes. My uncle, who also attended McPhail as a piano major, worked for his room and board at the Young Men's Residence Club on 3rd and 17th for two years. His job involved helping in the kitchen and waiting on the men who paid to live and eat there. As an unexpected fringe benefit, the club had a couple of pianos, so after completing school and dinner responsibilities at the club, he was able to practice without hiking back over to McPhail. The old stone buildings that formed the club have been converted to apartments rented by MCAD students and others just starting out in the big city-- many of whom might appreciate an opportunity to work for room and board if such an arrangement still existed.

As I became more intrigued with those board and room experiences of the past, I started looking for people to interview, and I discovered that the practice of working for room and board was widespread in small towns as well as cities. Richard Hall writes in this volume about working at his uncle's bait shop in Aitkin County during the summer of 1939. Jobs were scarce, Hall needed work experience to become employable, and his uncle didn't seem to mind the arrangement one bit.

Before school buses brought country kids into town, many farm kids who wanted to attend high school had to either find a room to rent or a place to work for room and board. Undoubtedly some employers exploited their workers and made them do an inordinate amount of work, but in many cases, the room and board arrangement worked well for both the boarder and the boardee. Boarders took care of children or helped with housework or outdoor chores. Food and shelter were currency, and no money exchanged hands.

Alice Henderson Fife was born in Beroun in 1927. Pine County had no school bus service, so kids who wanted to attend high school had to improvise. "I attended an eight-grade country school near our farm with one classmate, and we learned easily and finished two years early. My folks were concerned about where I would live when I went to town for high school because I was only 13 years old.

"During my freshman year, I stayed with my sister and cousin in one large room at my uncle's home. My sister graduated, and my grandmother moved in with her son, so I needed a new arrangement the next year. My uncle knew a family that wanted a live-in baby sitter. They had three daughters and one son ranging in age from seven years to three months, and my duties consisted of helping with the children, peeling potatoes, doing dishes and pitching in to help wherever help was needed. I had every other Sunday off.

"I never had my own room. I either slept in the girls' room or on a day bed in the dining room, but I never considered it a hardship. If there were school functions, I was free to attend. I walked about a half mile to school and home for lunch. In my junior year, I was in the class play and walked back to school for evening practice and home again in the dark.

"I was treated like one of the family, and I can remember going to Minnehaha Falls with them for a family picnic. I suppose I was there to help with the kids, but I was thrilled with the chance to go to the Twin Cities. During my second year there, I sometimes stayed alone with the kids when their parents went away for the weekend. I worked through the summer, again with every other Sunday off, and I often took one of the kids home with me on those Sundays. I stayed with them until I graduated. I don't know who profited more. They had cheap help, but I had a home away from home and an opportunity to attend high school."

A woman who asked to be identified as Mary had a more complex room and board story. After her mother died, her dad depended on her to help him on his farm near Freeborn. Her older sister, who lived in Albert Lea, thought Mary would have a better high school experience if she moved to the larger town and worked for her room and board, so at age 14 Mary moved off the farm and in with a town family that had three teenage sons.

They were nice people, she said, but they were having some problems. The mother did very little around the house, except to write an extensive list of chores for Mary. From the time she got home from school until her energy gave out, Mary had to cook dinner, bake bread, clean house, wash and iron clothes and do other heavy housework. With her extensive 4H background, she was proficient at many homemaking skills. Although the 16-year-old son helped her wipe dishes, he was free to do his homework while Mary worked all evening. By the time she went back to Freeborn at Christmas time, Mary was failing in school.

Mary complained to her father about her workload, and someone found her a new job taking care of a little girl whose mother worked downtown. Although she had to share a room with the little girl, her workload was lighter and more pleasant, and Mary had time for homework. At the end of that year, this second family no longer needed her services, but they recommended Mary to some friends who had two daughters.

The third job was heaven. Mary shared a room with one of the girls, did some housework, and was treated like family. The father promised to send Mary to college if she stayed with them, but then he died.

She stayed with the mother and daughters for a year after she graduated, until she got married, and they remained lifelong friends. Despite her shaky beginning, Mary looks back at working for her room and board as a positive experience.

If the actual practice of working for room and board still exists in today's world, the term is definitely used outside my hearing range. I'm not sure when the practice dropped off the radar screen, but I don't think kids do it anymore. They move in with roommates or share a house, but they don't often exchange servile labor for a roof over their heads and three square meals per day. Some might work as live-in baby sitters or au pairs, but they receive a salary and don't usually barter work for food and shelter. I think families occasionally still help out cousins or nieces with room and board arrangements, but I don't know how they work out the details.

With today's high cost of living, working for room and board would make sense as a way for young workers or students to establish themselves in a new community without laying out apartment expenses that include rent, damage deposit, furnishings, and utilities. But since we have become increasingly wary of unfair labor practices, liability, exploitation or sharing our homes with outsiders, the idea of working for room and board or hiring someone to work for room and board has become just another memory of simpler times.

Phy Ed
by Joan Claire Graham

In California they call it "phys ed," and in Maryland it's known as "P.E.," but Minnesota kids of my generation called it "phy ed." The Catholic school where I spent my first nine years interpreted the state requirement to provide physical education to all boys and girls somewhat loosely, and we called it recess. The nuns opened the doors and let us outside a couple of times every day, and we chose sides and played kickball or softball. When temperatures dropped and snow obliterated our playing fields, we stood around in tight groups listening to our teeth clatter and hoping we wouldn't freeze to death.

I heard from my public school friends about Ralph Summers, Albert Lea's elementary physical education coordinator who came around to their classes and showed kids how to build human pyramids and do jump rope criss crosses. The closest we came to anything like that was when Sister Jutta defied everything we had previously believed about nuns and rolled up her habit sleeves to pitch a kittenball to a ragtag bunch of fourth grade girls on St. Theodore's lower playground.

When we reached seventh grade, we moved over to St. Mary's Junior High, where there actually was a gym, and we were subjected to a some-what more formalized physical education program. But it was nothing like what they had in public school. We didn't even have to change out of our school clothes. Sister Capistran would herd us down to the gym or take us out to the playing field, where we chose sides and played kickball or softball. We sometimes played a game she called soccer, in which two equal teams lined up at opposite ends of the gym and numbered off. Sister put a big rubber ball in the middle, and when she called "3," the two players with that number burst from their lines and ran toward the ball and tried to kick it across the opposing line. The linesmen had to stay in place and provide defense by kicking the ball towards the middle.

That kicking was our most explosive way to let off steam at St. Mary's school, and with all our repression and adolescent angst, it's a wonder we didn't kill someone.

I remember one time when Sister called a number, two girls charged for the ball, and both missed and fell flat on their backs. I think of it whenever I see the Charlie Brown cartoon in which Lucy moves the football.

When I was in third grade, Susan Voigt, an older girl who lived next door, told me a story that provided the basis for my willingness to attend Catholic school though ninth grade--even with its all-round repression and lame phy ed program. She told me that junior high girls at the public school had to take a physical education class that required them to change into these crazy one-piece gym bloomers. And if that weren't bad enough, when the class was over, all the girls had to strip naked and take a shower in the company of the entire class in one big room.

I often see the world as divided into two groups-- those who don't mind exposing themselves in front of their peers and those who do. The former group consists mainly of males and the latter of females. Guys use urinals, whereas gals lock themselves into restroom cubicles. If the door on the cubicle doesn't work right, we'll move to a different cubicle. Gals spend hours in fitting rooms trying to find swimsuits that don't make us look like manatees, whereas males swim naked in some pools and don't seem to care if they look like Moby Dick. Men must have designed those communal showers in girls' locker rooms without consulting any females about this intrinsic difference between genders. Girls of my generation were extremely uptight about modesty, so the seventh grade shower was a traumatic experience that opposed everything we believed was right.

I remember Susan's exact words when I asked about her first group shower experience. "I've never seen so many bare naked people in all my life." The towels, she reported, were big enough to cover either front or back, top or bottom, take your pick. The teacher stood with a clipboard and checked off names of wet girls as they emerged from the shower. There was no escape except to confess to the teacher that you were having your period. Admit *that* to someone? The more I heard the worse it sounded. I couldn't for the life of me fathom who dreamed up such an obscene ritual, but I was glad to defer the experience.

But notice that I used the word "defer," instead of "avoid," because Catholic school ended after ninth grade, and state law required phy ed classes for both genders until the completion of grade ten. By the time I hopped into the community shower fray at age 15, the majority of my phy ed classmates had become somewhat inured to this strange experience of changing clothes in a locker room and showering en masse.

The summer before tenth grade, I received a letter from high school officials stating that an important change had been made concerning high school physical education for girls, and my heart leaped with hope. But as I read, my hopes sank into despair. No, they had not built individual shower stalls or eliminated the shower requirement; they had adopted the use of new gym uniforms and replaced the old bloomer with a modern outfit that could be purchased at J.C. Penneys. The new uniform consisted of a white shirt and dark blue shorts. The legs, about four inches long, had built-in elasticized color coordinated underwear to assure that if a girl were bending down to touch her toes, her real underpants would not show from behind. God forbid that the teacher and classmates who were soon to see you naked in the shower room would get a preview glimpse of the edge of your underpants.

My lack of enthusiasm for phy ed was based on reasons other than my aversion to group nudity. Changing from school to gym clothes was an ordeal in the middle of a school day. Girls wore girdles or garter belts, nylons, slips, dresses or skirts and blouses, and shoes--all of which had to be stripped off and shoved into a little locker and replaced with uniform, socks and tennis shoes. We were expected to complete this metamorphosis in about three minutes before lining up into squads that allowed the teacher to take attendance quickly.

We let our gym clothes grow rank before taking them home to wash, so the locker room reeked. The rule was that we had to get wet in the shower, and that's as much as we were willing to do. We got somewhat wet, but nobody felt uninhibited enough to scrub clean with soap before parading with tiny towel up to the teacher with her little clipboard. Getting dressed after the dreaded shower took more time than we actually were given, so we'd fudge on the towel dry and pay consequences. Pulling those girdles and nylons on in a steamy locker room over damp skin was almost impossible, and we'd sometimes race down the hall and show up for our next class more disheveled than it was acceptable to be.

Phy ed class met two or three times a week and alternated with choir or art. The girls' gym was a little downstairs dungeon that offered none of the amenities of the nicer boys' gym upstairs. Title IX was far in the future, and girls' programs and facilities were second rate or non existent.

There were no girls' teams in 1962, and almost the entire high school athletic budget was spent on boys. Girls could attend Girls' Recreation Association meetings after school or hope to be one of twelve selected as A-squad or B-squad cheerleaders. That was the extent of girls' sports at Albert Lea High School back in the days when at least 700 girls were enrolled. Diane "Sis" Knudson, definitely one of the most gifted athletes of my time, was allowed to scrimmage with the boys' tennis team, but was not allowed to compete. That was too bad because she would have given male competitors a run for their money.

Our phy ed class consisted of games, physical fitness exercises and tests, and learning the rules and scoring systems of football and bowling. We began the year with the football unit that culminated with a test. We played girls' basketball Iowa style with three forwards and three guards who could take only three steps with the ball and could not cross the center line. We learned how to bowl, took a few practice shots in the gym, and walked across Central Park to Town Club Lanes for the real thing.

We were allowed to wear school clothes and go upstairs to the hallowed and far more luxurious boys' gym for a square dancing unit with the boys. During one session, a squirrely boy from my group was summoned by Mr. Buhr to his office, where he was given a loud smack with what was euphemistically called the board of education, and I remember thinking that girls' phy ed wasn't all that bad. During winter we hauled out mats for gymnastics, but Kathy Rigby had nothing to worry about because our most airborne trick involved one girl lying on her back balancing another girl on her up-reaching arms and legs. A yearbook picture attests to the fact that no underpants were visible during the execution of this stunt.

I surprised myself by living through all of this. When I moved on to college I had to take six phy ed classes to satisfy my secondary teaching requirements, so I took general conditioning, a couple of dance classes and swimming.

Those classes also required written work and uniforms purchased at the campus bookstore. I tied big knots in the straps of my "one size fits all" nylon tricot tank swimsuit. All phy ed classes met two hours a week but only earned one credit, and it was almost impossible to get an A unless you were a phy ed major.

The biggest indication of progress and civility in my college phy ed program, however, was the presence of at least a dozen individual shower stalls with attached curtained changing booths. Apparently state college architects consulted the women in their lives about how women don't like to shower together in a big room with a row of spigots on the wall. College women did not have to bare-it-all in the company of strangers, so we actually took the opportunity to stay in our individual metal shower stalls and get clean, wash our hair, and even shave our legs if we felt like it.

I never became an athlete, by any stretch of the imagination. My response to athletic competitors is, "Go ahead and win if it's so important," and they hate that. I have stayed fit, however, and I still remember the basic football rules and how to score bowling, how to select a ball, and the four-step approach. I still don't like parading around in the buff, and I still don't think the group shower part of our school phy ed program had any benefit or was particularly well thought out.

Girls' and women's physical education programs have come a long way since I was in high school. Girls' sports are now allotted equal budgets, facilities, and press coverage. Girl athletes win the admiration of peers and parents and earn college scholarships to play basketball, soccer, field hockey, lacrosse, tennis, track and even ice hockey. Physical education classes in tennis, track, dancing or weight training are coeducational so both boys and girls use all facilities. Those dorky gym uniforms are gone. I don't think girls are as modest as we were forty years ago, but that's a moot point because mandatory group showers followed by traipsing naked past a teacher with a clipboard would be prohibited by even the most perverted and sadistic school administrators. Kids in Minnesota still call it phy ed however, and if they're like my generation, they'll remember the high and low points of phy ed class long after they've forgotten history facts, algebra formulas, or biology phylums.

The Tap Dance Kid Bites the Dust
by Joan Claire Graham

With the firm understanding that I would not under any circumstances be allowed to participate in the June recital, I was admitted to Mary Lou Regner's tap dancing class right after Easter in 1952. The Spartan room in the back of the first floor of the Hotel Albert contained the requisite dancing school barre and mirror, and from the moment I walked through the door, I loved the place, the teacher, the taps, the other dancers, the music, and the whole idea of being a tap dancer.

The tune was "Chicago, Chicago, That Toddlin' Town," and I caught on immediately to the tap steps. By the end of that first lesson I could do the entire dance the class had been working on for several months, with the exception of a tricky shuffle step hop shuffle step that I later mastered at home. Much to my delight, Mary Lou expressed surprise at my aptitude and said she thought I should dance in both her upcoming recitals in Albert Lea and Austin. Although I've dabbled in many artistic and academic areas, this was my first and only experience with instantaneous gratification and meteoric success.

My mother groused that Mary Lou used recorded music instead of a live pianist, but this was the only dancing class in town. Mary Lou discovered I could sing, so she asked me to sing "Chicago" in the recital. With no prior experience or inclination, I found myself suddenly thrust into show biz, and I loved it. My mother groused some more about having to make my costume, but I loved the costume. My only regret was that my tap shoes were white instead of black patent leather.

After that successful and intoxicating stage debut, I moved into a small tap group with three older girls, and we wowed crowds the next year with a comical "Sidewalks of New York" number. In addition to tapping, I sang a song when a little girl named Joyce danced. The next year, I paired off with Pam Schumaker and, at least in our proud parents' opinions, we became the Shirley Temple and Judy Garland of local tap dancing. We performed at several area events, and sometimes we car pooled with Joyce, a solo performer and another star pupil of Mary Lou's.

Pam and I danced for talent shows and service clubs and made our first television appearance on the cancer telethon in Rochester, but our big show business opportunity came when we appeared on the "Hemenway Talent Parade" in Austin. Undoubtedly the inspiration for "American Idol," the Talent Parade featured three local acts, and audience members sent postcard votes to determine which would reappear next week. I don't think there was any other prize.

We knew we were in trouble when we walked into the studio with our 45 RPM record, and the sound guy at the station told us their record player only played 78s. They called in a local pianist, who miraculously sprinted in on short notice, but she didn't have the sheet music for "Me and My Shadow" or know how to play it. Could we possibly do our dance to any other tune--one she knew by heart--possibly "The Syncopated Clock"?

"The Syncopated Clock" certainly didn't make sense with our "Me and My Shadow" choreography, but it was in 4/4 time and the pianist knew how to play it with two minutes until air time. Troupers that we were, we smiled and tapped our best taps and did our best to look confident while we danced to unfamiliar music on live television. Our hopes to win the competition were bolstered by the fact that the third act booked to perform that night failed to show up.

Despite our skill and obvious talent, voters cast their ballots for a pair of Austin girls who showed up with a 78 RPM record and lip-synched a song about a kitty in a basket. We received a nice letter of condolence from someone at the television station who told us the voting had been close, but that letter was no consolation.

Joan Graham and Pam Schumaker
The Tap Dance Kids

To be defeated in a two-act contest by a pair of girls pretending to sing shook my confidence and raised self doubt about my talent as a real tap dancer.

After that debacle, my tap dancing career quickly unraveled. Mary Lou closed her Albert Lea studio and invited us to attend lessons in Austin. Mom didn't drive, and my dad wouldn't think of driving me twenty miles each way for life-saving medical treatment, let alone dancing lessons. Pam's mom didn't want to drive that far either. The only tapper in our group who made the commute was Joyce. Joyce loved to dance, and her mother was willing to drive to Mankato, Austin, Waseca--wherever lessons were available.

I loved dancing too, but had no opportunity to continue lessons. A couple more dance studios that opened in Albert Lea while I was growing up folded quickly, usually without informing students. We'd show up a couple of times for lessons that never happened and conclude that the dancing school had closed. In the 80s I took lessons at Ozone and Minnesota Dance Theater in Minneapolis, but it was too late for this old dog to learn new tricks. I could always tap--do the steps--but that free spirit that allows a person to really open up and dance had been nipped in the bud.

But tap dancing gives me joy, and it's the kind of exercise I don't mind doing, so I thought I might find a place to take lessons in Albert Lea when I moved back to town in 2003. When I looked in the phone book yellow pages, I couldn't believe what I saw--an ad for Joyce's School of Dance. Could this be the same Joyce? Yes it was. Her dedication and her mother's willingness and determination to go the extra mile had paid off, and Joyce had been Albert Lea's resident dance teacher and civic theater choreographer for 38 years.

The supreme irony is that her long-established dance studio is located an easy two block walk from the house where I grew up back in those days when all the dance lessons I wanted to take were either short-lived or in other towns. But guess what? She doesn't teach adults. What a bummer! I guess it's not going to happen with me and tap dancing. Maybe I should take up another hobby--like writing books.

The Ice Rink
by Joan Claire Graham

The white leather figure skates my folks gave me for Christmas when I was 13 years old are still in pretty good shape. Satisfied that my feet had finally stopped growing, Mom and Dad sprang for a brand new pair that year. I had been satisfied to trade outgrown ones for the next size at the skate exchange at Montgomery Wards or Coast to Coast, but those new skates were beautiful, and I could hardly wait to get to the rink and show them off to my friends.

Everybody ice skated in Albert Lea when I was a kid. Some flooded rinks in their yards, kids who lived near the lake shoveled a clear spot, and the city flooded rinks at four parks. Hundreds of skaters crowded onto our public rinks during ice skating season, and newly arrived skaters sometimes had to wait their turn for a seat in the warming house where everyone changed into their skates.

Boys preferred black hockey skates or speed skates, and girls bought white figure skates and fastened colorful yarn pompons to the laces near the toe. Grandmothers knit heavy wool skating socks, mittens and caps, and we were glad to have them. My friends and I skated every day during Christmas vacation, all weekend, and occasionally in the evening under stars and lights.

I usually skated at Morin Park in Albert Lea, a six block walk from my house. A friend called a friend to arrange a skating date, a favorite winter activity. By the time we walked to the rink, with our skate laces tied together and hanging around the backs of our necks, we sometimes had to thaw out in the warming house before we took to the ice.

They no longer flood a rink at Morin Park, but that cinder block square warming house still sits there. Except for a small office in its southwest corner and two restrooms in the southeast corner, the warming house was one big room. A much- appreciated heater chugged away, rubber mats covered the floor, and benches lined the sides and formed back-to back rows down the center.

Under those benches sat a tangle of shoes and overshoes, all of which looked pretty much alike, so it was crucial to write your name on your overshoes and remember where you put them. A continuous flow of kids and a few adults made an unbelievable amount of noise in that warming house, despite frequent reminders by employees to keep it down.

Emerging from that warming house into cold, fresh air was invigorating and somewhat treacherous. Morin Park had a downhill slope from the warming house to the rink, and this ice ramp was always choppy, so after a bumpy downhill ride, it was a relief to reach the smooth, level rink. Radio music blared over loud speakers, adding to the ambiance.

When I was in third grade, the city recreation department hired someone to teach figure skating lessons. I attended all four lessons with one teacher and lots of kids circled around, and learned a move called the Mohawk. The Mohawk involved two forward steps, a turn, a couple of backward steps, a crossover, and an arabesque, but in many years of watching Olympic figure skating I don't think I've ever heard that trick mentioned. Besides the Mohawk, nobody who frequented the public rinks knew how to do many fancy moves, so we generally skated forward or backward in a counter-clockwise circle, which added up to a fair amount of exercise because Morin Park's ice rink was almost a block long. A hockey rink on the north side was off limits to recreational skaters.

While we skated round and round, mile after mile, we socialized. Rowdy kids sometimes organized illegal games of crack the whip, and once in a while a chase ensued after a boy grabbed a girl's scarf or hat and took off with it. We heard rumors about which girl liked which boy, and sometimes there would be a sort of courtship dance on ice. He'd skate by and turn, and maybe skate some circles around the girl, and she'd straighten up and try to look especially fine while putting on a great pretense of ignoring him.

Evening skating under the lights held great romantic tension and possibility because after dark it was unusual for boys and girls to be in a social situation that was this loosely chaperoned. If you were lucky, the guy who had been skating circles around you might take your hand and ask you to skate around the rink with him. Of course, you would be too self conscious to conduct much of a conversation, and he would gladly drop you off to rejoin his friends after a round or two. It would be nothing really, except the topic of conversations for days to come.

Freezing was part of the game. Skaters would hobble up the incline into the warming house, where they would force their frozen fingers to remove skates and massage toes that ached from the cold. Thawed out, they'd put their skates back on and head for the rink again. Eventually, when fatigue or time got the best of us, we'd take off our skates, tie laces together, put the laces around the backs of our necks, and start walking home.

The first few steps without skates seemed weird because on solid ground with shoes and overshoes, we felt short, earth-bound, slow, and leaden. Walking home we'd review the day's events at the rink and freeze our fingers, toes and noses one more time. Moms would caution kids not to track in too much snow and issue reminders to put wet coats, hats, snow pants and socks on the radiator or near the register to dry. I can still smell that wet wool.

What a bargain ice skating was! A walk to the rink followed by a couple of hours skating kept us socialized, out of our mothers' way, busy, and physically fit. We burned a lot of calories and slept well afterwards. For the cost of a pair of skates, new or used, we enjoyed about three months of serious recreation every year.

High school homework and other social activities pulled older teens away from ice skating, which might explain why my last pair of skates is still in pretty good shape. But maybe the popularity of recreational ice skating was on the decline by the time I reached that age.

The last time I skated on a public rink was in Robbinsdale in the early '80s. When my daughters were little, we used to bundle them up after supper and pull their sled over to Lee playground, where we all skated. From a new perspective I watched young teens still doing those courting dances on ice, but the crowd had grown very sparse.

Many towns, including Albert Lea, now have figure skating clubs where a relatively small number of kids pay quite a large amount of money to skate indoors and learn the intricacies of figure skating, and both boys and girls now play high school hockey. Those activities involve adult supervision and organization along with significant financial and time commitments, so by their nature they exclude non-competitive, recreational, spontaneous participation by the masses.

The city still floods a couple of outdoor rinks in Albert Lea, but I never see many skaters. On a brilliantly cold Minnesota Sunday afternoon, while a few kids are being coached to play hockey or do remarkable spins and jumps for upcoming shows and competitions at an indoor skating facility, the masses who used to simply have fun outdoors, flirting, exercising and socializing while skating around in unremarkable circles, are sitting home watching televised sports and eating chips. Some might call this progress, but I call it a shame.

I've Been Working on the Railroad
by Joan Claire Graham

When Howard Fife talks about his job, his eyes light up, his energy quickens, and stories of disaster, heroism, hard work, humor and adventure spill out with great enthusiasm. He knows that his stories hold details that can only be relayed by a railroad man. He has so many stories it's difficult to pick just one to preserve for posterity, but the over-all interesting story is that of Howard himself. He worked for the same company for 40 years, loved his work, and is excited by the prospect of sharing some stories that made his work memorable. I sometimes have to stop and ask what he means because like all professions, railroad work has some unique vocabulary.

His home is decorated with railroad memorabilia and a telephone that rings with the sound of a train whistle. He worked for Great Northern Railroad, and after more than twenty years of retirement, he still meets fellow retirees for lunch once a month. Although they talk about the present, it's not unusual to retell stories of remarkable events they witnessed on the job. They saw the railroad industry prosper and fall, and though their work was tough, they loved what they did, and they lament the decline of railroads in America.

"For a hundred years there's been a Fife on the railroad. My dad was a boomer, a guy who worked for several railroads. He went to work on the Great Northern in 1918, and I wanted to work where my dad worked. So on August 27, 1942, I hired out on the Great Northern Railroad. We are a family of railroad men. My son started working there in '67, and pretty soon he will retire."

Fife interrupted his career with a three-year Army hitch, and by the time he got home from the war, railroads had nearly completed a transformation. Diesel engines, which could be doubled and quadrupled to pull heavier loads and longer trains, had replaced steam engines, thereby laying off boilermakers and other shop workers. But the upsurge in peacetime manufacturing kept railroads busy shipping materials and goods to a nation eager to get going again after wartime conservation.

Fife spent his early years in the freight house loading boxcars from semi-trailers. In 1949 he told his superintendent that he wanted to work in the switching yard. "At first they told me there were no vacancies, but when I threatened to quit, they caved in and told me I had a switching job. I hired out as a switch helper, and the next year I was made switch foreman. I worked in the Union Yard over by the University."

The switchman's job was to disconnect the engine and some cars, divert them onto side tracks, and connect new cars bound for another destination. An eight-hour shift typically dealt with six to eight trains, and trains ran 24 hours a day. Weather and fatigue augmented the inherent danger of managing the connections and disconnections of thousands of tons of rolling steel, and mistakes could be costly in every sense of the word.

 The switch yard was a dangerous and busy place where it was not uncommon for workers to lose limbs as well as lives. Howard Fife had a couple of close calls, and he bears a lump on his hand where two boxcar couplings pinched it. Doctors wanted to take his thumb off, but he wouldn't let them. His injury proved to be a clean break so they put his arm in a cast, and the injury healed well.

Some of his true stories would set movie audiences on the edges of their seats if they were portrayed in action adventure films. "In 1965 there was a big explosion by the yard. Everyone ran down the tracks and saw that it was a boxcar that blew up. I turned the air valve and gave the engineer a signal to pull away, but the engineer had abandoned ship, so I had to move the engine. The boxcar just melted from the heat caused by chemicals that were intended to be used for something in the paper manufacturing process--to bleach wood pulp. The cloud caused by the fire contained so much bleach that it bleached the boxcars pale. It started making pock marks on my skin so I went to the hospital, and they gave me a vinegar bath to counteract the acid that was on me.

"The train master who was on duty hadn't liked me, but because I had managed to separate the burning car from the rest of the train, I prevented three more cars from similarly burning. Who knows how much damage all those toxic clouds would have caused? The master liked me after that. I was his hero.

"In the late '50s, the supervisor called me to work a yard job at 11 p.m. on Christmas Eve. I told him I wanted to stay home with my kids so I said I would come in at 1 a.m. I showed up, and they told me to go down to the yard, grab a track and pull it out. I went down to get the cars to switch out. The engineer pulled out, and I pulled out the hand brakes. After I took the first bunch of cars that they pulled off, I was going to put the brake down, and I threw my knee out of joint. That paralyzed me, and I threw myself onto the tracks and started yelling for help.

"This drunk guy saw me and started yelling, 'Man with a leg off!' They came to pick me up on a stretcher, and the canvas ripped right down the center. I told them to lift me up on the poles, with one leg and one arm over each pole. They took me down to the ambulance. My knee was out of joint, but the doctors snapped it back into place."

Although his own accidents bore relatively minor consequences, Fife saw his share of tragedy in the switching yard. "Smokey Barland, another switchman, had half his leg cut off. They were trying to put a tourniquet on his leg. I grabbed his blood vessels and held them while they called an ambulance. I couldn't let go because my hand was cramped shut. They put me in the ambulance with Smokey and gave me something to unclench my hand. Smokey took it hard, and never came back to work.

"Another guy had his arm and collar bone ripped out. His wife left him, but when he received a big settlement she came back and wanted to share it. We'd sometimes find bodies in boxcars or along the tracks. Sometimes it was an accident and sometimes not."

Stories resulting in loss of life or limb would spread among all the guys who worked for the railroad, as would the stories of mishaps that resulted in lost time or money.

"On my second week on the job, I watched a passenger train pull out of the station after I gave them the highball. As the cars rolled by I saw one with the wrong logo on it. That train would have taken passengers on the wrong route if I hadn't caught it. They had to stop, back up and reconnect. That was the biggest mistake I remember as a switch helper.

He tells another favorite story to demonstrate how railroad men understood each other and made allowances for human error. " We were on western lead–the tracks on the other side of the main line. I was instructed to shove some cars back, so I told the guy to push the cars back far enough so we would have enough room.

"We were on track 2, and we took cars off 1 & 2 and got 45 cars together. We went to the engine to pick the rear men up. As we were pulling away, the engineer detected trouble. I grabbed the throttle and opened it wide up. As it went faster and faster, the engineer kept saying, 'Something is wrong, Howie.' But we didn't know what it was.

"We slowed down, and when we were shoving up the main line, the yard clerk said, 'Look at the mess you made over there, Howie.'

"I said, 'I have all my cars on the track; don't kid me.'

"He said, 'Go over and look.'

"I did, and he was right about the mess. We had pulled up 45 car-lengths of track– all torn up.   When the hind car hit the switch, it went on the ground and pulled up the track and ties at the complete end of that track. When it hit the west end of the track, it jumped back on the rail again. I made out an accident report thinking, 'How can I get out of this?'

"When we finished the day's work, I saw the train master and said, 'I don't know if it was Stan or myself who caused the accident.' He recommended I bring in a union rep, but I confessed. He gave me five days suspension, but gave me those suspension days on my days off, so I didn't get docked any money. He told me to watch my nose from then on. That accident caused a lot of financial consequences for the railroad, so it was good that the person doling out my penalty was an understanding guy."

The railroad made mistakes too, and Howard loves to tell how he helped prove that point. "In 1973 I came to work at 7 a.m. They had a terrible accident in which a guy had one leg cut off. The railroad officials had a safety meeting for all us day men. They started blaming this accident on the guy who was hurt. I said, 'We have safety breaches that I've reported.'

"They said, 'Everything you've reported has been fixed.' Then the yard master made an announcement to hurry up and make up for lost time.

"I said to the safety guys, 'There you are. You tell us to hurry, and you wonder why we have accidents.'

"They told me to go down and make a cut–separate cars and open the air valves. I turned the air valves–angle cocks–and saw some broken planking that I had previously reported. I fell on the ground on purpose. The engineer came and said, 'How bad is it Howie?'

"I said, 'Make it look good.'

"The yard master said, 'Attention everybody, we have another wounded guy coming up the main line.'

"They called the ambulance, and when I got on the ambulance, a guy whose lawn mower I'd fixed said, 'Can I have your lawn mower?' I was faking it.

"When I got to the hospital, I started walking and hopping around. The doctor said he should take an x- ray, but I told him that nothing was wrong. The train master picked me up. When we started back up the road, I got out to check the broken planking, and it was all repaired. The yard master sent us all home, and this time everything really was fixed."

Howard's stories seem endless, but another remarkable one had to do with dunnage, a term I had never heard. Dunnage is anything that's left after a freight car has been unloaded, and it can include packing materials and cardboard as well as wood from crates. It was common practice to burn this material, but it was okay for workers to salvage and recycle anything they wanted to keep.

"I built a cabin out of dunnage. When I saw a guy starting a fire with some 2 x 4s out by the tracks I shouted, 'Stop! You're burning my porch!' I actually built my whole place from stuff that would have been thrown away." His wife Alice nods to verify the authenticity of this tale.

While reflecting on his career, Howard Fife expresses only one regret. "It was a great job. I got lots of exercise, I got along with fellow workers, and I loved what I did. They used to pay us to go to a good-time meeting with management so they could get our input." His sole regret concerns the demise of the railroad industry, and he shakes his head as he relates his disappointment.

"In their heyday railroads employed two million people in this country. Small towns had station agents, and the depot that proudly bore the town's name was a busy place that handled mail, milk, grain and passengers. Trains don't even stop in most small towns now, and their depots have either been converted to other uses, torn down or left to decay.

"None of the yards I worked at is still in existence. Today in this entire country there aren't even two hundred thousand railroad jobs. Great Northern in Minneapolis used to employ as many people as all the railroads in Minnesota employ today. The only railroad left in Minnesota is the Burlington Northern Santa Fe. They haul huge loads of potash, coal, and grain nonstop. Their money maker is container cars--two high and filled with goods from China and Japan. Most ground freight is hauled by truck."

Howard Fife's string of stories finally winds down for the evening, but his final career assessment packs a punch at a time when job discontent and career switching are so common in the American work force. "I worked on the railroad from 1942 until 1982. I loved my job. If I had it all to do again, I'd do it exactly the same way. It was an honor to go to work on the Great Northern Railroad."

Howard Fife

The Cowpie
by Anita Kieffer Poss

It was a hot day on the farm in 1949-- sticky hot. As Bobby and I stood barefoot, leaning against the old barn with the sun beating down on our heads, I could see the sweat beads on Bobby's face. The edge of his hair hung in damp clumps, and a smear of dust clung to his cheek.

We watched the old hen come scratching around the corner. She pecked at a black bug uncovered with her last scratch. The hen had been clucking around the big old barn for days. Bobby and I knew she was sitting on a nest in the hayloft. The hayloft was trouble because Mama said it was dangerous. Still Bobby and I sneaked up to check on the eggs. The first time we found the nest, there were only four eggs nestled in the hay. Whenever we could, we would snitch an egg from the chicken coop and add it to the old hen's stash. Now nine eggs lay in her nest, along with a couple feathers and some soft white down.

That morning, while Mama was hanging clothes on the line, Bobby and I swiped another egg. It was smooth and warm in my hand as I carried it to the nest. Bobby and I were waiting to see if the old hen would notice it. The hen stopped in front of the barn door to roll in the fine gray dust of a dried-up mud puddle. She shook her body clean, then clucked herself through the dark opening of the barn. Bobby and I slowly inched our way in behind her as the hot air hung heavy with no breeze from outside. The steady buzzing of flies droned in our ears. Bobby started up the ladder to the loft, and I followed closely behind. We had to be very quiet, or the old hen would start squawking and raising a fuss. Mama would make us go in the house if she heard that old hen squawking.

Slowly we eased up the ladder. Over the edge of the hay we could see the hen, but she wasn't sitting on her nest. She was circling around making a low clucking sound. Bobby climbed onto the slippery mound of hay. He stretched his neck for a better look as he crawled closer to the nest. Suddenly he started yelling! I could see his outstretched hands grabbing in the air, trying to grasp the hay, but he kept slipping toward the edge of the loft. Feet first, Bobby fell screaming to the barn floor below. The startled old hen was flopping and flying, bouncing around and squawking madly.

I scurried down the ladder to find Bobby sitting on the floor staring at his foot in amazement. He had landed on a board with a big rusty spike in it. The spike had run through the sole of his bare foot and was poking out the top! Bobby looked at me, then back at his foot and started screaming.

I ran yelling for Mama. I was barely out of the barn when she came running across the yard toward us. She rushed past me wildly looking for Bobby; she saw his foot and gasped! Mama yanked at the board, but it wouldn't budge. She yanked again and again. Finally it broke loose and the spike came out. Bobby stopped screaming and started to whimper. Mama's face was as gray as a rainy day in summer as she studied Bobby's foot. Frantically she turned to me saying, "Run to Mrs. Wisher's. Call Grandpa. Tell him to come. We've got to get Bobby to the doctor."

I was gone--past the yard and down the curve of the driveway, my heart pounding in my chest. I passed the willows near the rock pile and turned on the main road, a straight run to Mrs. Wisher's. By the time I sped past the cattails where Bobby and I waded in the cold ditch water, my lungs were aching. On I went, past the woods and wheat field. The sweat poured down my face as I passed the crossroads. Mrs. Wisher's gladiolus were waving below her kitchen window just beyond the next rock pile.

Rap! Rap! Rap! I knocked on her door. Finally it opened, and she called Grandpa on the telephone. He was on his way, and he would take Bobby to the doctor.

Back at home, Bobby lay on the couch with his foot propped high on pillows. The doctor had given him a shot. "Keep his foot elevated. No playing till the swelling goes down." Three days passed, and the foot was still nasty, all puffed up like a football. Bluish gray and green faded in and out of the tightly stretched skin. Mama was worried, and she was chewing her lip like she always did when something was wrong.

Bobby didn't want to color or play Old Maid anymore. He was watching a fly trail across the windowpane behind the couch. He wouldn't listen to the radio or read my Little Lulu comic books. The fly flew away. As Bobby turned his head, a tear rolled down his cheek. He didn't want to talk. He wanted his foot to be better.

The screen door banged behind me as I walked down to the barn to pet the cats. The old hen wasn't scratching around, and I didn't go in the barn to find her. I sat near the open door and let the kittens crawl in and out of my lap. A quiet breeze whispered through the air. Pigeon grass waved against my leg, tickling ever so slightly. Bobby's foot was awful, and he couldn't play. Mama cat strolled by and meowed, and her kittens scuttled off, following her into the barn. As I started back to the house, kicking a stone along the path, Mama came out the door carrying Bobby. "We're going to Grandma's to see about this foot," she said.

Grandma was baking gingerbread, and the sweet, spicy smell escaped through the open kitchen window. Uncle George had just come in from the field with Grandpa. He stood at the water pail with the dipper uplifted to his mouth, his Adam's apple jumping at each big gulp. Grandpa wiped the dust from his face with his blue print handkerchief. They all turned to look at Bobby as Mama set him on the kitchen table. "Look at the size of his foot," said Grandma. "It needs a cowpie plaster."

Uncle George and I hurried to the barn to collect a scoop shovel. Leaving the farmyard, we headed for the pasture beyond the south 40. The cows were grazing in the late afternoon sun, and their bells gave an occasional clang as they lumbered toward thicker green patches. A cow was pleasantly lying, chewing her cud as Uncle George nudged her in the haunches. She didn't move. He gave her a harder shove, and this time she arose and lifted her tail. Quickly Uncle George stuck the shovel behind her to catch the cowpie before it hit the ground.

As we raced back to the farmhouse with the steamy catch on the shovel, Grandpa and Grandma were waiting on the porch. Bobby was sitting on a chair, his foot in a white enamel dishpan, and Mama was pacing back and forth across the porch.

Grandma opened a brown paper sack as Uncle George ran up the steps. He dumped the cowpie into the sack, and Bobby's eyes grew large as Grandma stuck his foot far down into it. Bobby's mouth opened but no sounds came out as Grandma placed his foot in the cowpie sack back into the pan. With a piece of twine, she tied the sack shut around Bobby's knee.

Bobby found his voice and let out a mighty shriek. "Now, Bobby," said Grandma, "we have to get rid of that poison." Bobby slouched in his chair, with his arms crossed, a pout dragging his lower lip out. Grandma opened the screen door and remarked, "Better watch that lip or you'll be tripping on it." The door slid shut behind her.

I sat on the porch waiting...and waiting...and waiting. Occasionally, Grandma came out to check the sack. Finally she appeared with a pail of warm, sudsy water. She washed Bobby's foot, which had shrunk back to normal size. Cautiously he stood and took a couple of steps. The foot was fine, good as new.

In the evening, Bobby and I went down to the barn to play with the kittens. As we sat in the quiet dusk, the old hen came sauntering past. Following closely behind her were four fluffy yellow chicks.

Bobby and I haven't played in the hayloft for over 50 years. Still, we remember the chickens, the cats, and the sweet smells. We remember the big rusty spike...and the cowpie.

Anita Kieffer Poss presents story time at the Campbell Library in East Grand Forks, where she lives with her husband Nicholas. They have five children and ten grandchildren.

Anita Kieffer, 1949
When the story took place

Early Years in Stillwater
by Ella Lindner Arsenault

My mother must have worked hard at making me feel wanted and loved. I don't doubt that I was loved, but I learned in later years that I was really not wanted. My mother wanted a boy and was so disappointed when I turned out to be a girl that she wouldn't look at me. The name she had chosen for me if I did turn out to be a girl was Audrey.

My Aunt Ella was staying with my mother before and after I was born. She and my mother fought like cats and dogs, so it made no sense that I was named after her. The midwife said that since Ella was the first one to hold me, I should be named for her. As a matter of fact, there was no name on my birth certificate--just "Baby Girl Lindner." Since my mother had so desperately wanted a boy, she didn't care what I was named.

Mother got over her initial disappointment so thoroughly that I only learned of it later from my older sister Flora. I recall a happy childhood, and my mother was very much a part of all those memories. I was raised with Flora and my much older brother Herman in Stillwater, where we moved when I was a baby after my dad got a job as a toolmaker at the state prison in 1909. We first lived on Maple Street and then moved to a nice house on West Myrtle Street and Owen.

We had a summer kitchen off the back of the house where my mother washed clothes and cooked during the summer. My father had a work bench with tools out there, and we stored stove wood there too. When they decided to add indoor plumbing, my parents dug a cesspool on the summer porch, and the thought of falling into that deep hole--even though it had a cover on it--scared me when I was little.

My sanctuary was a swing outside our back door. One Sunday I spent a whole morning swinging and crying because one of my favorite comic strip characters, Dolly Dimples, had disappointed her friend Bobby by going off to play with someone else. I felt so sorry for Bobby that I was beside myself. Finally my mother came out to find out what was wrong with me and try to comfort me, telling me it was just a funny paper. I never felt quite the same about Dolly Dimples after that.

I was pretty much of a cry baby during my younger years. My mother used to tell how I cried all the time when I was a baby. She said she had to carry me around on her hip while she did her work because I cried as soon as she put me down. Maybe I felt rejected. Mother told me that when Flora first saw me she said, "Take her away." My brother was an awful tease. I guess they weren't happy about having a sister either.

We had lots of friends to play with on Myrtle Street. Arvilla Johnson was my best friend, and we walked to school together every day. She and I and my sister Flora used to play with nickel dolls, which were small breakable china dolls with movable arms and legs fastened with elastic. My father always replaced the elastic cord with wire so it wouldn't break.

Since the dolls were only four or five inches tall, we could easily use Mother's sewing scraps to make clothes for the nickel dolls. We made carriages out of match boxes. These boxes came in a wooden container that had a slide-on top. We fashioned a buggy top, put the nickel dolls inside, and pulled the carriages around with strings. We called on each other with our doll families and had lots of fun. Flora became very skilled at making doll clothes, and she was generous about giving them away. One Christmas my mother burned the midnight oil--and it was really oil because we didn't have electricity--an sewed beautiful coats and dresses for our nickel dolls. I think we played with those dolls until we were 12 years old.

The streetcar went by our house, and there was a single track. If we knelt down and put an ear to the track, we could hear if the street car was coming. Then we would put pins on the track and form them into different shapes. The streetcar wheels would flatten them out to look like scissors, boats or whatever shaped thing we could figure out.

Stillwater had its share of strange town characters. One was Fisherman John, who used to drag for bodies of people who had drowned. Though he never let anyone watch his operations, which he conducted at night, he was so successful that he was sent for from all over the country. Another man, named Gabbert, could neither see, speak or hear. He hung around the pool hall and could understand when fellows wrote on his hand.

On the north hill a dirty bearded man we all called Snappy Johnson walked around with a small wheelbarrow picking up junk. He was bent over, and when the kids saw him they yelled, "Snappy bulldog bite," and he would chase after them. I never yelled at him because I was too scared.

On Saturday nights my sister, mother, father and I would walk down to a movie--we always called it a show. It was a long walk--maybe ten or twelve blocks, and the trip home was up a long steep hill, and sometimes my dad ended up carrying me. Every Sunday my mother dressed us up in our pretty dresses, and at 4 p.m. we'd wait outside Carlson's store. When the doors opened, we'd each have a nickel to spend on ice cream or candy.

When I was in first grade, I developed an abscess on the right side of my neck. My mother took me to the doctor to have it lanced, and when he lanced it my mother had to hold the basin because he didn't have a nurse. A different doctor in Lake Elmo told mother to open the abscess every morning with a darning needle. She would lay me on the dining table and go at it. I was scared stiff and told her to use the blunt end of the needle. I was out of school for six weeks, and my parents had my picture taken because they thought I might die.

Of course, I didn't die. I went on to lead a very long and rich life. Many years after my childhood in Stillwater, at the encouragement of my children and grandchildren, I wrote some of the things I remembered of my growing up years. It was not meant to be a history of my life, but it was interesting to see how much things had changed over the years, and interesting to see how a little girl started out as a disappointment to her mother and ended up doing pretty well in her life.

Ella Linder circa 1928

Ella Arsenault died in 1999 at age 90. She had four children, 18 grandchildren and 21 great-grandchildren. This is an excerpt from her book, So Be It, submitted by her daughter, Mary Silberschatz.

Leek Lake Lodge
by Jeffrey L. Cardinal

Even before I was married I knew of the cottage in Minnesota officially called Leek Lake Lodge, located deep in the woods just a few miles from Detroit Lakes and Vergas. It was a simple cottage, with a kitchen and a small bedroom with partition and a drape to separate it from the rest of the living area, The living and dining rooms were combined. For a long time the biffy in the far back of the property was the only toilet facility, and its path was euphemistically called "the road to cut-foot lodge."

Water had to be pumped out back and carried in for washing and bathing. This retreat in the northern woods of Minnesota was where my wife and my in-laws from Ann Arbor, Michigan, spent a month each year. The length of time spent there was dictated by the academic calendar that affected my father-in-law, Bob and my wife, Liz. He was on the University faculty, and she was a student. My mother-in-law Miriam had a somewhat more flexible schedule, and she was always glad to make the trip. The cottage was a place were the Butsch family was linked by common experiences, and it represented a bond to Minnesota roots. They always brought along a dog or two, so after they stopped in Owatonna to pick up my wife's grandmother, Josephine Butsch, the car was pretty full.

Bob and his dad, Al Butsch, bought the cottage around 1948. Before that they rented other cottages in that area. It was a place where Bob and his father could avidly pursue their fishing. Not long after buying the cottage, Bob did his doctoral research in zoology in a woods nearby, studying the individual home range of the red-backed vole.

Besides enjoying the out-of-doors, Bob and Al loved fishing, and Bob did photography which he used for reference when he built dioramas and exhibits for The Exhibit Museum at The University of Michigan. Bob and his father searched the lake for the best spots for catching fish, a practice Bob continued through the years. They mainly caught pike, large mouth bass, rock bass and sunfish. To my great surprise, my mother-in-law Miriam enjoyed going fishing with either Bob or Al. In my family, the women stayed away from worms and slimy fish.

Bob kept extensive records of each day's fishing, noting the location of the catch, the kind of fish, the water and air temperature, along with other information he thought was relevant. Bob's mother Josephine did not fish, mainly because causal clothes did not suit her Edwardian sensibilities. She enjoyed a tour of the lake in the boat once a year.

When Liz was 17, she caught her biggest fish ever, and it rivaled any that her dad caught over the years. Liz felt a big tug, and it was obvious she had a big fish on her line. It didn't take long to realize she had a northern because it didn't act like any bass she'd ever caught. It took at least a half hour to play and reel it in. All through the process her father encouraged and offered advice like, "Reel in; let out the line a little."

When they finally got it into the boat they realized why the struggle had been so fierce. The northern pike measured 36 inches and weighed 12 pounds. They wanted official statistics so they went over to the resort nearby to weigh and measure it. Bob made an outline of the pike on a piece of heavy paper, and somebody took a picture of Liz and her fish. There would have been no way to keep it and have Bob make a cast of it when they got home so they ate it, and it was very good, according to Liz.

I heard many times about Liz and her father using the five-gallon cement mixer to make stepping stones along the side of the cottage and a walkway from the front of the cottage out to the biffy. This was a long, laborious project because you can't make much cement in a five-gallon mixer with no running water! This project provided Liz a wonderful opportunity to be with her father. She loved the things he did– fishing, wildlife, and traipsing through the woods.

One year as they drove to the cottage, Bob quizzed her on identifying birds, because she had decided to take an ornithology course at the University of Michigan Biological Station "Bug Camp."

Liz always spent her summers up at the cottage on Leek Lake. It was a place like many children have where summers are best spent and new experiences are around the corner--doing something out of the ordinary, which feels ordinary. Her first summer away from the cottage was when she was in college on an archeological dig in Missouri. Each time she received a letter from her folks at the cottage, she wished she was there.

It was not until the mid 70s that my in-laws made any modern additions or renovations to the cottage. They built a bedroom and a large bathroom, mainly to accommodate Josephine's age and make it possible for me to use the cottage. A ramp in front was built for both of us, and to my surprise, there was a new dock 36 inches wide to facilitate my wheelchair.

In 1979, Liz and I were able to make a trip to the cottage. It was a two to three day drive, depending how you wanted to break it up. We made the usual stop in Owatonna to visit with Liz's grandmother Josephine, who was still living in an apartment on Broadway above Cashman's Florist Shop, where she and Al had lived. Owatonna reminded me of many small towns I had visited with its comfortable and easy going, down-to-earth people.We continued north the next day. As we went farther north past St. Cloud, it looked much like northern Michigan to me. Lines of trees along the interstate indicated that the road had been cut through the forest.

As we headed down one of the wide gravel roads to the cottage, it became all very familiar to Liz. Rounding a corner, Liz intuitively pointed to the gate we had to go through, down a two-lane path. Farther down through the trees was a reddish log cottage with shutters varnished to their natural wood color. It was nestled underneath the trees sitting high above the lake. For Liz, it looked as it had when she was last there.

The walls and vaulted ceiling were paneled in knotty cedar, finished in a warm honey color. The knotholes created designs to ponder, and there was a stone fireplace. Everything about it said "cottage in the woods." Over the fireplace hung a deer head, and snowshoes crossed on the wall. At the front window was a very small table made of white pine. On it was a welcoming note written on birch bark and a map of the lake with notations of the best places to try catching fish. It felt like home, a place to relax. Liz and I spent two weeks there. We fished, played cards, read and relaxed. I bought my fishing license in Vergas at a multipurpose hardware store where kitchen items, toys and various other things could be purchased. We swam and took turns fishing, and enjoyed watching new loon chicks and beaver over on one side of the lake. To Bob's record book we added our notations, which now made me a part of the cottage's history.

I was also be able to add a fish story. One night spin casting near the Bradbury shore, an area that was noted on the map, I caught the biggest (and only) large mouth bass I ever caught– 2 pounds, 14 inches long. We took pictures to validate my fish story. We named the road down to the dock "the bonsai pipe line." I would get up so much momentum in my wheelchair that Liz would jump on its back pipes as we rushed down.

On our way home we headed north so we could travel through the upper peninsula of Michigan. We passed through Bemidji, Hibbing, and Duluth and other Minnesota towns whose names I'd heard.

I became part of the lore of the cottage in Minnesota, feeling as much a part of it as Liz. I met the Shrupps, who looked after the cottage for Bob- -two of the nicest people I have ever met. They epitomized most people from Minnesota--gracious, self-effacing, kind, and willing to make you feel like family. We visited two more times, making a trip to the head waters of the Mississippi, and then missed the cottage greatly as the years went by. To me the cottage felt just like the one I knew as a boy in Michigan—with the north Minnesota country holding something special.

In 1984 Bob and Miriam decided to sell Leek Lake Lodge for practical reasons. Josephine's health was failing, and she no longer lived in Minnesota. The drive seemed longer each year, and they wanted a place that was closer for grandchildren and Liz and me. I believe that selling the place was a very hard decision to make. They took many things to their new cottage, but many things had to be left behind. However, this small cottage, Leek Lake Lodge, in the northern woods of Minnesota, held memories we all still treasure and a tie to the North Star State.

Jeffrey L. Cardinal is a freelance writer in East Lansing, Michigan. He is the author and publisher of Time Lines...A Collection of Short Stories.

The Wedding Dress
by Betty Jean Rueckert Collins

When my daughter Terri Jean came home from Phoenix to Minnesota Lake one weekend in June of 1996, she had to chew the foot she had previously put into her mouth. Some time ago she had told her sister that whenever she got married, she would make her wedding dress, and Heike Jo had called Terri Jean on this promise. For an entire weekend we were literally on pins and needles as our family became a wedding dress production line. Even though it was hectic, we gals really had fun together.

Heike Jo failed Sewing 101. Terri, who excelled in this craft, found a Butterick pattern with a scoop neck and straight skirt as the starting point, although the design wasn't really what either had in mind. Terri Jean had a vision of how she could transform it into a wedding dress by redrawing the pattern to resemble a party dress pictured in *Modern Bride* magazine.

Heike Jo and her friend Jean Renner drove to the Twin Cities and proudly returned with a very special package of fabric they'd purchased for $50. The urgency to make this important purchase and sew the dress was prompted by Heike Jo's plan to leave the nest, take flight, and move to Oklahoma. The chosen fabric sat waiting on Grandma's spare bed until Terri Jean arrived from Arizona on June 22. In a matter of hours, she was to magically and lovingly turn it into a wedding dress.

Now the fun began. Sunday morning started with Terri sitting in a yoga posture in the middle of Grandma's living room floor, eyes closed and meditating, trying to capture a vision of how to overhaul the Butterick pattern. Pacing the floor, I thought we'd never get started. "Come on, Terri," I said, "we only have two days, and time is getting away from us."

"I'm still thinking," was all the satisfaction I got from my nervous urging. I didn't want to be left holding the bag and having to go it alone on this project. I stopped sewing many years earlier, when my daughters realized the existence of store-bought clothes and rummage sale castoffs.

Finally, a breakthrough. "Grandma, do you have any paper?"

"Ummmm," Grandma replied, pausing to think a minute, "let me see. Yes," we heard as she headed down the hallway and returned from bedroom number two. "Will this work?"   "Perfect. Thanks Grandma."

Grandma had some old rolls of used but clean shelf paper that once covered flower stands at Festag Days' Hortag show. Being a product of the dust bowl, Great Depression, and World War II, she felt it was a shame to waste anything holding potential future use. "I often wondered why I saved this paper. It's a good thing I did."

With the skirt pattern pieces laid out on paper in the middle of Grandma's living room floor, Terri Jean, still sitting cross-legged, took up her pencil and concentrated on transferring the flare and flow of her vision onto paper. "Grandma," she began with an 'I know you must have it' tone in her voice, "do you happen to have an old sheet?"

"Well, let me take a look." Grandma disappeared into the back bedroom and searched successfully for a retired sheet, which again was rated perfect by the meditative seamstress/designer. Terri cut and sewed a test-run dress out of that old sheet, and made note to make this seam bigger, take a tuck here and there, lengthen this and shorten that until we all wagered the final dress would work out just right.

With her revamped pattern cut, Terry Jean pinned it to the real white satin and brocade. "My gosh girl, aren't you going to test out this idea first?" I asked in shock.

"Never mind," she answered confidently. "Trust me, it'll work." Trust me. Trust me, I tried to reassure myself with skepticism, worry, and downright fear.

The living room was a disaster with the ironing board on one end, all the shelf paper and scraps in the middle, and a box of pins, randomly forgotten, sitting somewhere in the middle of the clutter. The card table sat within an arm's reach of the extended dining room table that we converted into a cutting station. We took our positions. Terri Jean manned the scissors, and I settled in at the card table that held the sewing machine.

And Grandma....well, she was kind of a cheerleader from the sidelines. She vacillated from the hassock to the couch or whichever direction she was pacing to and from to give her rousing cheer, "It'll never work. You should have left it the way it was."

As Terri Jean handed me carefully cut fabric, piece by piece and seam by seam her vision of a perfect dress for her only sister emerged into a simple wedding gown. My skepticism turned to optimism as the dress took shape. There was the lining yet to make and a hidden zipper to put in. Oh that zipper! We sorta made our own rules sewing these separate units together into one, as it was all on-the-job learning as we went along.

Every once in a while Grandma would share her "You should have left it the way it was" cheer, and I made peace by reminding her that we had to trust the project engineer, Terri Jean. Besides, we didn't have any more fabric, so it had to work out. She supported the project by ironing fabric and seams.

Since both sisters were the exact same size, we figured that fitting the dress to Terri would assure her sister of a perfect fit. We made a small allowance for unforeseen irregularities by allowing some adjustment of the ribbon belt in the Empire waist. In our final assessment, we felt she would have to take whatever she got, but with love we gave it our best.

We made many trips forth and back to the floor-length mirror at the end of the hall. On one pass through the clutter I inadvertently stepped on that open box of pins, scattering them galley-west, and our cheerleader was right there. "Go on. This is my job; I'll pick up pins," was her new cry as Terri Jean and I made our trip down the hall to the mirror for another reality check.

By Monday evening it looked like a real dress, complete with zipper and lining, and it all hung from a plant hanger in Grandma's dining room. We were feeling pride in our accomplishment of the past two days. Terri Jean had a dinner date with her dad so she had to leave for awhile. Grandma had another errand, so I was left alone to finalize hem pinning. The plant hanger served a mighty useful function as I lay supine on the floor beneath the dress.

The lining had some problems so after calling Heike Jo to check for measurement discrepancies, I swallowed the lump in my throat and closed the scissor blades to cut excess lining fabric. It turned out to be the final cut.

Terri Jean got us to the finish line in less than two and a half days before we drove her to Minneapolis to board her plane back to Phoenix. The rest, now up to Grandma to finish before her forthcoming cataract surgery, was to hand sew the lining and hem. By July 13, the dress was done.

Now in Oklahoma, Heike Jo, experienced a pre-wedding panic attack. Facing the prospect of not trying on her dress until the day before her wedding, she called me a bit frazzled. She asked me–implored me–to Fed-Ex the dress ASAP so she could be certain. "I have only six weeks before the wedding, and I have to know. I want it to be perfect."

Fed-Ex next day service wanted $57—a bit more than the cost of the fabric, so we sent the dress via UPS for a mere $18. I figured she could manage her crisis for three or four extra days.

The wedding went off without a hitch later that summer, and a photograph taken that day of the bride surrounded by her bridal gown family work crew attests to her happiness. Her sister, grandmother and I were proud and happy we had all pulled together to make her a unique and memorable wedding gift.

Betty Jean Collins, a retired nurse, is happy that both daughters have moved back to Minnesota. Terri Jean Kidd Hoffart lives in Good Thunder, and Heiki Jo Dodge lives in St. Cloud. Betty Jean and her husband Tom moved from Wells to a farm near Minnesota Lake in 2003.

Hall Hockey
by David Chrz

In 1965 I was a freshman at St Mary's College in Winona. I lived on the fourth floor of Heffron Hall, the oldest building on campus, built in the days before it became popular to build educational facilities with complicated floor plans. All the hallways were just straight shots, with double stairways centered along one wall and a single, multi-paned window above a radiator at either end. The floors were made of beautiful red slate tiles.

A lot of my fellow students were hockey players. While waiting impatiently for intramural hockey season to start, some guys got the brainstorm to take the fire hose from the wall between the stairways and flood the floor with water, making those slate tiles as slick as ice. Then, sliding around in bare feet, they had full-blown hockey games, with a goalie posted in front of the radiator at either end of the hallway. A metallic "bonggg!" signaled a goal. Unfortunately, a "crash! tinkle, tinkle" signaled a broken window pane, and these were scored at a rate of about two-to-one to goals, as some yahoo fired off a slap shot from center "ice."

Eventually the lakes and rinks froze over, and our hall counselors, Rick Kurz and Charlie Nash, posted a notice for all interested parties to attend a meeting forming an intramural hockey team- "special equipment will be issued." The season had arrived at last! No dummies Kurz and Nash, the attendees were all pretty much the hall hockey players.

After a brief meeting, the new intramural hockey team from Fourth Floor Heffron emerged from the counselors' office. Their "special equipment" consisted of buckets, cleanser, and Brillo pads. Their first game was scheduled for that very afternoon, against the hundreds of black marks left by pucks and taped sticks during their hall hockey matches. Charlie Nash had even opted for a "coach" sweatshirt and whistle, which he sounded vigorously during the game in that closed, resonant hallway. Those poor saps had never seen restitution coming until it was too late, and we watched our hall counselors out of the corners of our eyes with new-found respect for the rest of freshman year.

Austin native David Chrz lives in Abilene, Texas.

Wedding Day Blizzard
by Alta Doyscher

Many Minnesotans are familiar with the Armistice Day storm of 1940. The storm I most vividly remember, however, is one that occurred in January of 1927. That storm threatened my wedding plans and became a memorable backdrop for one of the most important days in my life.

I met Matt when we were children in Jackson. Matt's sister worked for my mom, who thought Matt was great. I was 15 years old, and I fell in love with this boy who was four years older. My mother died when I was 16, and I went to live with my married sister Roselle in Minneapolis. Matt and I drifted apart, and when I came back to Jackson before my senior year, Matt was engaged to another girl. We rekindled our relationship, however, and during that summer he and I got back together. He had completed his barber's training, but he still needed to take his state boards.

I went back to my sister's house in Minneapolis, and after high school graduation I got my own room in Minneapolis and went to beauty school. In the meantime, Matt got a job in a Hollandale barbershop, even though he wouldn't be able to take his certification test until May. Matt and I set our wedding date for January 28, 1927.

Since we lived a hundred miles apart, and since neither of us had a car, getting together always required strategy and planning, and our wedding day was no exception. Matt's friend was supposed to drive Matt to Clarks Grove on January 27 so he could stay there in a hotel and catch an early morning bus to Minneapolis. By the time they started out from Hollandale, snow was falling so heavily that they had a hard time getting to Clarks Grove. Snowdrifts blocked the road, but Matt and his friends went to heroic lengths to ensure that our wedding would not have to be postponed. They had to repeatedly get out and push the car through snow, and by the time Matt reached the Clarks Grove hotel, he was soaked to the skin and chilled to the bone.

He never did dry out, and he couldn't sleep in his wet clothes. When morning arrived, he was disappointed to learn that the weather had made the road impassable, and that his bus would not be arriving to take him to Minneapolis. Of course, he had no way to call and tell his bride this bad news, so even though the weather was terrible, I didn't know that our wedding day plans had hit a snag. In a mood of excitement and anticipation, I took the Bryant Johnson streetcar to the bus depot to meet my groom. When I arrived at the depot, they told me, "No busses will arrive today because of the storm." You can imagine my disappointment.

Meanwhile, back in Clarks Grove, weather conditions improved somewhat, and Matt discovered that one bus was going to attempt the trip to Minneapolis on those snowy roads, so he got on it. I don't remember how I got word, but I got back on the streetcar and met that bus when he got into town. By this time, it was already late afternoon. Our wedding time was quickly approaching, and we had to hurry to get ready.

I had just enough time to get dressed and go over to my sister's house. I changed into my beautiful, sheer, champagne-colored short dress with a dropped waistline and long sleeves. At $35, it was quite an extravagance--but after all, this was my wedding gown. There was no time to go to a photography studio, so there were no wedding photographs taken that day.

The minister and his wife came to my sister's house on McKinley in Northeast Minneapolis for a 5 p.m. wedding, followed by dinner. After they left, Matt said, "We're going dancing," so we went out on the snow-packed city streets and found a dancing place. It wasn't a formal wedding dance, but it was memorable. After the dance we went back to my rented room.

The next day we got on a streetcar to get to the depot to take a train to Jackson. We had some wedding photos taken there, but we thought they were so bad that we didn't save them. A few days later we came home to Hollandale. We couldn't afford a house, and there was no apartment to rent so we found a sleeping room with a single bed. Since we were newlyweds, we didn't mind.

In May Matt passed his exam, and we bought our first car, a Ford coupe. I inherited some money so we bought a little cottage that we moved and remodeled.

We eventually moved to Albert Lea and bought a big house on Clark Street, but Matt commuted to his barbershop in Hollandale until he retired in the 1970s. We were married 65 years and had four daughters, ten grand-children, and eleven great-grandchildren. Over the years, they enjoyed hearing the story about the snow storm that tried unsuccessfully to delay our wedding day in 1927, and I enjoyed telling it.

Alta and Matt Doyscher, the young bride and groom.

Alta Doyscher ran a catering business in Albert Lea for more than 20 years. She enjoys baking cookies and rolls to share with her neighbors at Thorne Crest Retirement Center. She celebrated her 95th birthday in August of 2003 in the company of 147 friends and relatives.

Hollandale's Little Rascals
by Donna Doyscher Hawkinson

Hollandale was a small town with no crime, no traffic, no deadbeats, no child molesters – just a great place to grow up and live. There really wasn't much to do except to FIND stuff to occupy our time, and sometimes I found myself in trouble.

When I was about five or six years old, Bobby Wagner and I played together a lot. His mother, Bertha ran the Home Cafe, the only cafe in town. Bobby was one year younger than I, and he was fun. He always had great ideas of where to ride our bikes or how to get into trouble. He also could sneak a package of gum from the candy case, and one time he took a pack of cigarettes and invited me to go down to the ditch, sit under the bridge, and smoke. We rode our bikes down there, but Russell Madden, the depot agent, was outside talking to the railroad guys, and we decided we'd get caught because Russ knew our parents. So we went back to downtown Hollandale and tried to figure out how to smoke our cigarettes.

Across the street from the cafe and Dad's barbershop we saw a culvert– one of those big ones that would be put under a driveway when they got around to digging it in. We decided to crawl through it--just because it was there. Bobby went through first. Then I started. I could see the hole at the end, and Bobby was looking into it saying, "Hurry up, come on…"

I must have panicked because all of a sudden, I was halfway through and I couldn't move. I couldn't go backward or forward. Oh God, I am being punished for planning to smoke a cigarette. I told Bobby to run and get Dad from the shop because I couldn't move.

Dad came, and I can see him so clearly, peering into that culvert. It was afternoon, sunny, and the contrast of the light and his wonderful face was burned into my memory. He said, "Well now, if you got in that far, you can sure get out. The pipe isn't any smaller at this end than it is at that end. You can do it . Come on, I'll just wait here for you." It was such a relief that Dad was there I relaxed, began to "shrink" and crawled out.

No, we didn't smoke cigarettes that day!

Probably a year after the previous episode, Sylvia Anderson and I decided to go across the road and visit Paul D. Jones. He owned the marketing company that shipped onions and potatoes all over the country. He was rich, he was a gentleman, he liked kids, he knew my folks, and he always allowed us to come into his office and say "hi" and then go on about our business.

Christy Christenson, his office assistant, also was a great, friendly guy who would always kneel down when he saw me on the sidewalk and say, "How's my little redheaded friend?"

This particular sunny afternoon, we decided to take a walk around the big warehouses and play. Then we both had to go to the bathroom. I wonder why we didn't just go across the road to Sylvia's house, but we didn't. We went into the outhouse that the warehouse men used. In 1936 most employers didn't provide indoor bathrooms for hired help--not even Paul D. Jones!

We went inside, hooked the door of course, and sat down. I won't go into detail, but anyone who has ever used a REAL outhouse knows what a two-holer is like. When it came time to leave, we couldn't get the door unhooked. We poked and pushed and poked again until our fingers were bleeding from pushing on the point of the hook. It was just too tight.

There were only two solutions to this problem. We either would have to go down through the hole where we could see a little sunlight, (Oh God!! No!!) or call for help. We agreed that calling for help was the best idea. I yelled at the top of my lungs, "Christy, Christy, Christy, Christy…" for what seemed like hours. We waited, thought again about solution #2 (a terrible pun) and then I started yelling, "Christy, it's Donna – Sylvia and I are locked in the toilet – please come and get us out." We both were crying because we thought we would die in there and that no one would even miss us.

Finally, there he was. A man who heard me yelling had gone to the office and gotten Christy, who then came and somehow jerked the door open so we could get out. He wasn't smiling though.

He told us we should have known better, and he said he was thinking about calling the constable (that was what Hollandale had instead of a policeman). I had NEVER seen Christy mad before, and I was scared to death! He promised not to tell Dad if I would promise to never do such a stupid thing again. I promised!!

You would think I'd have learned my lesson, but I continued to get myself into predicaments. Vic Tostenson's house was cream-colored, with dark brown vertical trim on all the corners, and I decided it was a wonderful place to use my colored chalk. It was right next to our driveway, and in a small town people aren't outside watching what the neighbor kids are doing unless it's noisy, destructive, illegal, or obviously wrong. I wrote with my chalk, all the way up as far as I could on the brown siding . Oh, what fun! Then I went over to the other corner, and wrote on that brown siding as well. Soon, Vic's whole house was decorated with my yellow chalk writings.

Just after supper, Vic came to our door and said, "Who the hell wrote all over my house with yellow chalk? Whoever did it better get over there and clean it up."

I got "the look" from Dad, who had just finished eating, and I admitted that I had done it and it was "just a little chalk." Well, I took a bucket of water, soap and a sponge over there, and not only did I have to wash off the chalk, but I had to go a little farther and wash the entire siding as far up as I could reach. It took me all that evening and the next day to finish.

Another summer afternoon Marilyn Tostenson and I were playing at the Central Elementary School playground. We were swinging and wondering what to do with the rest of the day when one of us – I don't remember who – suggested that it would be fun to get into the school, since there was no one there, and investigate all the nooks and crannies that we didn't get to go into when school was in session.

We tried one window that opened to the back of the stage in the basement, and it wasn't locked! So what would be wrong with just going in? It wasn't locked, so we wouldn't be breaking in, would we?

We were totally alone in that school, and it was the eeriest feeling I have ever had. It was exciting because we knew we shouldn't be there, and we knew we could get caught if someone happened to see us. We left the same way we got in, but as we were climbing out of the window, Mrs. Lambertus, who lived across the road, saw us and yelled something that sounded like, "I'm going to call the police," (but we HAD no police!) and we ran like a couple of greyhounds to get out of there as fast as we could. Whew! That was a close call. I don't think anyone ever found out about it, and neither of us told our parents, as I remember.

I still think of those childhood days in Hollandale very often and remember all the fun we had. We had wonderful adventures on those lazy summer days – and we really weren't BAD kids.

My sister Alyce was 7 and I was 5 when this was taken at our Hollandale home.

Donna Doyscher grew up in Hollandale, lived in Hoyt Lakes for 23 years, then moved to Clearwater, Florida in 1980 where she and husband Ray reside

Dirtdrifts
by Alyce "Penny" Jacobsen

We Minnesotans all know about snowdrifts, but those of us who lived in southern Minnesota during the 1930s remember dirtdrifts.

Novels and movies like *The Grapes of Wrath* tell about the dustbowl years in Oklahoma and other plains states, but Minnesotans had a similar problem during that same era. My strongest memory of this phenomenon is of trying to keep the dirt--actually fertile, valuable, vegetable-growing soil--out of our house in Hollandale. For several years there was practically no rain, and the soil was extremely dry.

We lived at the east edge of Hollandale, just across the road from a 2-acre onion field. There were no buildings or trees to discourage the south wind from moving dirt from Sam DeHaan's field to our front yard. Black drifts, just like snowdrifts, decorated our lawn during the late springs and early summers of 1933 and '34.

I was only 6 years old in 1934--young enough so that my memories of those hardships are somewhat hazy, but old enough (at least in my mother's judgment) to help keep the house clean. I should say that we tried to clean the house, because it was an impossible assignment.

The blowing dirt was composed of very fine particles--peat decomposed to what was known as muck--and it penetrated the tiniest entry areas. Doors and windows could not keep it out. Mother put wet newspapers in window sills, stuffed wet rags around windows, and put damp rugs against the doors. On windy days, they were black within minutes. We kept wet rags handy, and wiped off any surface we were going to use or sit on. A small, hand-held vacuum got lots of use and had to be emptied several times a day. Cleaning was never-ending.

Our dining area was located just inside the south-facing windows, and it was a challenge to have a meal without eating too much dirt. We placed plates and cups upside down and wrapped silverware in a napkin until the very last minute.

On windy days, playing outside was impossible, and Mother postponed doing laundry until a calm day. For weeks, she had to hang clothes inside. Dad usually walked to work at his barbershop three blocks away. Some days he walked with a wet handkerchief tied over his nose and mouth. On the worst days, he drove, and when he came home for lunch he would park the car right by the door, wait for a lull, then dash inside.

Occasionally the drifts of dirt in the front yard were so big that Dad had to get rid of them. He shoveled muck into pails, put the pails into my wagon, hauled them across the street and put the farmer's soil back in the field where it came from. For my family, dirtdrifts in the yard and in the windowsills were a frustrating mess and an inconvenience. But for many farmers who watched their seed and topsoil blow away, those dry years spelled disaster.

My memory must have been aided by stories I heard throughout the years I lived in Hollandale. Whenever someone complained about dry, dusty weather, we'd hear, "You should have seen what it was like in '33 and '34."

Alyce grew up in Hollandale, attended college in her 40s, and worked as a speech and language clinician in Glenville, Emmons and New Richland schools. Now retired, she lives with her husband Earl in Albert Lea.

Dirt storm near Hollandale, 1934

Hanging on to a Piece of Wilderness
by Alyce "Penny" Jacobsen

My family has a piece of wilderness that we have enjoyed for 43 years. It has pine and hardwood forest, a meadow, a meandering river, limestone bluffs, fossils and wildflowers. In late April and May there are many places where you cannot walk without treading on bluebells, trout lilies, or spring beauties. In fall, the golden leaf carpet rustles, but if you stand still and there are no birds about, the place has oceans of silence.

Owning a piece of wilderness happened because one evening in 1959, Orv and Alice Gilmore were discussing with us the farm land surrounding Albert Lea. Someone said, "Isn't it a shame that so many farmers are cutting down their wood lots?"

We agreed and said, "Maybe we could buy a few acres of woods and keep it natural--make a sanctuary for wildlife." Two other couples, Nelsons and Birdseys, were also interested.

So our search began. We hiked through several potential "briar patches" near Albert Lea and rejected them: too expensive, too close to traffic, no access road, or not for sale.

We knew of a valley in Fillmore County that had all the features we wanted and more. Maud and Joe Koevenig had a cabin near Spring Valley, and Maud wrote glowingly about the area in her Tribune column. An adjoining acreage had just come on the market. We saw the place--120 acres and an old cabin--on a mild November day, and we were fascinated. The road, or trail, led down a steep slope, then through the river before heading into dense woods and on to an open grassland rimmed with bluffs. Our feeling was, "If we like it in November, surely we will love it in other seasons. And it's only an hour's drive from home. Let's buy it!"

After months of negotiations with an elderly owner who did not really want to sell even though we offered his full asking price, we finally closed the deal by giving him lifetime use of his favorite hillside. The four couples divided the land.

Gilmores bought 60 acres including the cabin, and the other three families got 20 acres each. We drew lots to see which family would own each of the 20-acre parcels. Birdseys got turtle ponds, long views of river and cliff, and the earliest hepaticas. Nelsons got most of the meadow, the deepest part of the river and an excellent cliff view. We got some of all the best--trees, river, cliffs, fossil beds and flowers, even a resident red-tailed hawk, in the most secluded corner. Each family would pay their own taxes, mark trails, cut firewood and make changes only on their own land, but we agreed that all of us could hike and enjoy the scenery on the whole 120 acres.

Over the years we picnicked, camped, fished a little, waded and raced homemade boats. The biggest hill was wonderful for sledding and skiing, and some winters we used snowshoes to get around in the valley. All of us searched for fossils, frogs, turtles and snakes, and we learned a lot about birds and wildflowers. Our sons helped plant, trim and harvest Christmas trees, created stepping-stone routes across the river, and built tree houses, grouse feeding stations, and even a split-rail fence as a special project in 1976. Early in January of most years we'd have a "picnic in the snow." On a sunny day, sheltered by a south-facing limestone cliff, it could be quite comfortable. Hot dogs never tasted better.

We controlled weeds and grasses by renting part of the property for pasture. We learned a lot about cows too. They not only leave lots of free fertilizer, they are curious and will lick cars and picnic gear left unattended. The pasture rent paid the taxes.

Most of the time it was possible--even fun--to drive a car or pickup through the river, but during high water, or in winter when the river was partially frozen, we faced a challenge getting to our part of the valley. Sometimes we left the vehicle at the top of the hill and walked or snowshoed to our picnic spot. Jake had hip boots, and for several springs during flood season he carried me piggy-back across the river. Then, for Mothers' Day in 1973, my gift from him was a pair of hip boots.

Often, Jake would wade through the river crossing to determine whether or not it was safe to drive through. Twice we got stuck. Once I walked to a nearby farm, and a neighbor came with his tractor to rescue us. But one time the Mercedes got river water in the wrong place and we needed a tow truck. High water or low, we always told the kids, "Watch out for alligators."

We shared the valley with friends, relatives, scouts, Audubon groups and Thorne Crest residents. Seniors from Mother's retirement center loved the opportunity to experience a little wilderness. Hazel, a frail 86-year old woman who walked between able-bodied helpers, stood in the river in borrowed hip boots with tears of joy running down her cheeks. "I thought I'd never ever get a chance to be in the woods again until I got to heaven."

Buying "a piece of wilderness" was the best possible investment. For about $1400 in 1960, our woodland acreage has provided us with all these years of pleasure.

Now, in 2004, things have changed. Sons have moved too far away to visit the valley. Original partners have sold and moved. New owners have cut down healthy trees, mowed the meadow and hillsides, and built bridges in an effort to tame the wilderness. There are still deer and turkeys, but fewer birds. One of these years Jake and I will have to decide. Is it time to sell? Or should we wait for one more wildflower season?

Alyce Penny Jacobsen picnics in the snow.

Coming to America
by Tena Broesder

Because I was left handed, I had to fight for everything. First my father and then my teachers ridiculed and punished me for using my left hand. When I started school, I knew how to write all my numbers, but when the teacher saw me using my left hand, she took away my slate, slapped me and shook me. The knitting teacher ripped out every stitch I made left handed and made me start over. By the end of first grade I was using my right hand.

Even though my teenage brothers Ben and Klaas had traveled across the ocean to help our uncle farm in Minnesota, the rest of my family was content to stay in Holland in 1913. My father and mother worked hard every day to provide food and shelter for us five girls: Harmke, Geertje, Emegie, Trientje, and Martje.

Farming the old way was back breaking, as horses were only used for hauling, seeding, harrowing and hauling the crop in. The rest of the work was done by people, bent over. The boer (boss farmer) hired our parents by the year, with house and garden available. There was rent to pay at the end of the year when a new agreement was made.

Money was always running short, so Mother and Dad were looking ahead. At ages 45 and 39 they felt they were getting older and the work would never be lighter. My brothers in America had rented land near Adrian, and they wanted the rest of us to join them. My parents finally broke the news to their parents and to us girls that we were going to America.

My older sisters protested because they didn't want to leave their boyfriends, their bicycle, or their jobs, but Dad had the last word. We sold most of our household goods, our livestock, our sacks of potatoes, our everyday clothes, and our lovely hanging lamp with crystals hanging around its globe. Some things were packed in wooden crates. Mother cried as we left our house early in the afternoon. After spending that first night at Grandma's house, we boarded the train to Rotterdam. We had never even seen a train before! Grandma, who was seeing her eighth child leave for America, kissed Mother as we left and said, "Don't forget me."

We arrived very close to the harbor, where we saw a beautiful liner, the *New Rotterdam*. As a marine band dressed in white played Holland native songs on the second class deck that warm March afternoon, we were taken to the very bottom of the ship to our third class cabins. Second class was for people with money, and those folks would not be examined when we reached Ellis Island.

Even if it was third class, it was spotless in every way. The meals were good, and nobody complained. There was accordion and mouth organ music going late into the night, and at least 50 young people would dance, walk around and get acquainted. We tasted popcorn for the first time, and we liked it. At some point we decided our Dutch names would have to change, so we became Hattie, Gertie, Emma, Tena and Martha, and our last name changed from De Lange to DeLong.

Hattie at age 16 was at her best, flirting and very pretty with her brown hair combed high and fastened with a comb, and most men wanted to dance with her. At 14 Gertie also started becoming sociable. Second class people came down to dance, but we were not allowed to go up to their deck. Dad became worried. Mother and I played cards and ate treats.

After we left the English Channel, our ship gained speed and waves grew higher. The second day out, Mother, Emma, Martha and I got so seasick we didn't leave the cabin for days. Dad had to look after us and keep his eye on the two teenagers. A storm made the pitching of the ship even worse, but finally we felt better. But now Gertie got sick. She complained of hot flashes and couldn't leave her bed, though good times were going on as before. The porter sent a doctor who said that Gertie would have to be taken to the hospital, and two sailors in white took her away on a stretcher. After two days we heard nothing about her.

By then we had arrived in the New York Harbor amidst much excitement as the Statue of Liberty came into sight, but we had heavy hearts because we were worried about Gertie. All our friends passed their physical exams on Ellis Island, and we were told where to catch the train. We were headed for Adrian where, as someone on the first day of our long ocean trip had told me, there would be Indians who would scalp us.

Gertie went to a hospital in New York, and we didn't know if she was alive or dead. A Holland minister came to our little group to help us out. He told Dad to change our train ticket, for they had decided that it would be best for Hattie to stay in New York so she could be at Gertie's side. We couldn't do much but agree to go along with it, even though the girls were both young and didn't know English or how to get along in New York.

The minister said he would look after Hattie, so we said goodbye, and Dad exchanged gilders for dollars. We took a taxi to Grand Central Station, where passenger trains lined up. We managed to find the right train, and for two days and nights we ate apples, pies, and other snacks sold in the aisles of the train. After switching to another train, we finally arrived at the depot in Adrian at 6 a.m.

My brothers and uncle had met every train coming from the east for many days and nights. Finally the station agent said he would notify them if anyone strange to him arrived. A snowstorm had caused drifts so high that roads were only open to bobsleds, so there we were on that cold morning. The station agent got us to come into the depot. He talked to us, but we did not understand. After what seemed like a long time three men bundled in full-length sheepskin coats, overshoes, caps and gloves drove up, and we were so overcome to see familiar faces...and so were they.

Our strong boys had rented an acreage with a set of old farm buildings with cottonwood trees and much garden around. The house was ugly brown with large glaring windows with no shades, but inside was a new stove with lots of trim and a nice oven. There were closets, a western type crank washing machine, a wash boiler, milk pails, pots and pans and a kitchen table with ten round back chairs. Billy Bofenkamp, the hardware merchant in Ellsworth, helped the boys accumulate all these things. There was coal, cobs, flour and other grocery staples. Those blessed boys.......

Later we bought two milk cows, and friends brought potatoes, a bit of meat, and plenty of lard. We had five or six hens for eggs, plus a rooster, and in time we had enough roosters to make chicken soup. Our crates of freight arrived, but no word came about Hattie and Gertie.

Eventually we learned their whole story. After we left New York and the minister, Hattie had been found unconscious on a bench, cold, hungry and soiled. A welfare worker found her and took her to a hospital, leaving her coat, suitcase and ticket behind. She was diagnosed with encephalitis, so sick that she was not even able to identify herself for four weeks. Gertie, in the meantime, got back on her feet, and with her bright red hair and good looks, she got to be the nurses' pet at a different hospital. They put ribbons in her hair and they brought clothes for her because she left the ship with nothing but a nightgown.

Nobody knew what to do about the two girls, and then one day Hattie's coat was found, and in the pocket they found a note that told which hospital Gertie had been taken to. Much to their surprise and delight, the two girls were reunited, and the wheels started turning. Hattie now wore a dust cap because her beautiful hair had fallen out.

But the girls were together again, and they boarded a train to join the family in Adrian six weeks after the rest of us had arrived. Our brother Ben picked them up at the depot and drove them in his new buggy and his best team of blacks to our farm. What a reunion it was, although Dad was working for daily wages at a nearby farm. Gertie was healthy and strong, and Hattie wore her dust cap. Both wore strange clothes that had been given to them by hospital workers. We were family again.

To our dismay there was no water on our place, only an old cistern caved in, where the water was lifted up by pail. Though Ben was farming, Klaas went working on the railroad. He gave his pony and buggy to Dad so he could make trips to work and haul drinking water.

Lucky Martha was too young, and Gertie and Hattie were too old, but school was torture for me and Emma. Dad's boss was on the school board, and he insisted we go. The first day we acted brave and carried our lunch in a sack. We saw that it was a mistake because all the other kids carried their lunch in syrup pails. We had a few of those, but not knowing the local custom we took our lunch in paper sacks. That was boo-boo number one. It was April, and everyone came barefoot. We wore our best shoes. That was boo-boo number two. The other kids wore patched overalls, and we didn't. That was boo-boo number three.

The teacher was a pleasant young girl somewhat surprised to see new pupils. There was no way to get through to us because we didn't understand the language, but they found a place for us to sit as all eyes focused on us. The teacher played the organ and school opened with a song. We wondered what would come next as a piece of paper and a pencil were handed to us. We understood to write our names and ages, but we didn't know what else they expected. The class giggled and went on with their routine. At recess we were teased, and the teacher asked many more questions that we were unable to answer.

The next day an older girl came to help us. She spoke a German-like language which was hard for us to understand, but between her and the teacher they got our history and an idea of what grades we had completed in Holland. Emma and I both knew our multiplication tables through 12, but we could not read or understand much. By the end of the term we were doing a little better, and we attended the school picnic.

Although our brothers were big, strapping men, they both worked away from home. We girls were willing workers, helping Mother in the garden and wherever else we were needed. Hattie's hair grew back, and Gertie got a job for $2 a week. Were we happy? Perhaps, somewhat.

This country was bountiful, and prices were high, so Dad decided we should start farming the next year. Eighteen-year-old Ben stopped at the Adrian First National Bank and asked Charlie Fitzpatrick if we could have a loan if a chance came up for us to get a farm. Charlie pointed out an upcoming September auction and said the bank would help in any way.

Ben drove over to that place, on a good gravel road, and learned that the owner was selling out to move up to the Red River Valley. Dad and Ben attended the auction and bought the 40 acres with green corn in the field, all the hay, a team of horses, some cows and sows, a buggy with two seats, and a cream separator.

Owning a farm meant a big change, and Klaas now stayed with us. Mother gave birth to a baby sister, which was a joy and a surprise. Eventually our 40 acres proved too small so we rented 160 acres across the way because we needed to raise livestock feed for the long winter. That year A freight train going west spit out smoke and sparks, setting fire to our hay-stacks and cornfield. Section men were called out to fight the fire well into the night as it spread out a half mile and burned everything in its way.

Ben learned of a 400 acre farm for rent west of town, and we moved there in 1917. Hattie worked as a maid for a lawyer in town, and Gertie worked for a farm family with five children. Klaas married, and Ben ran the farm and joined a bunch of men known as the Nobles County Guard. They had uniforms and practiced with guns and stood on guard whenever called upon. During the war we never heard a word from Holland.

After the war there were happy days when farm prices held up for some time, so there was money to buy all those things we desired and needed, for life on the farm was hard in every way. We loved our lovely place and took care of everything. It was by no means modern, but we did not know that. The pride we took in doing our best gave everyone a boost.

Eventually Ben and my older sisters married, and in 1923, when I was 20, I married Caspar Broesder. We rented a one-story bungalow with a barn, and I had saved so much money from doing housework that I could almost pay for whatever we needed. We were married almost 60 years, and we raised six children in Nobles County.

After a busy life, I am now what is known as a senior citizen, and I manage very well with simple surroundings and my circle of friends. It has been an eventful trip for the little girl who was born left-handed in Holland. I've faced many challenges, seen a world of change and progress, and experienced many ups and downs, but I have many happy memories.

Tena Broesder lived in her own little red house in Adrian and enjoyed planting gardens and sharing their bounty with her neighbors until she was 88 years old. She died in 1992.

Farm Work and Fun
by Bonnie Broesder Hauser

Farm kids of my generation did have fun, but hard work went with it. We six kids lived on farms near Adrian and Lismore in Nobles County, and our parents, Tena and Caspar Broesder, let us play all afternoon, but first things came first. We had to work all morning.

Mom had a big garden, and she canned everything that could be canned. We pitched in to help, and to this day, I use her recipes for pickles and beets. We spent many mornings pulling weeds in the garden and out in the corn fields with Mom right there beside us. The worse field job was shocking grain, How we hated that, but again Mom was right there.

We loved to see the threshing machine and hay wagons, and we would sit by the roadside watching the procession come to our house. I was driving the tractor by the time I was 11 years old, helping Dad harvest oats. Dad had a rope from the binder to the tractor clutch, so when there was trouble, all he had to do was pull the rope and everything stopped. We girls had to pitch in because by the time he was a teenager, my older brother Bill was working away from home on a crew that followed the wheat harvest from south to north. Mom used to tell Dad that he was taking her hired girl with him to the fields.

We all had to milk cows, except for Mom, who was afraid of them. My first experience with milking was when I was about 9 years old. I guess the cow didn't like me because she sat right down on her rear when I tried to milk her. We pail-fed calves who liked to suck on our fingers. We girls didn't have much to do with pigs, but Mom knew how to slop the hogs. We had to chop wood for fires and also gather corn cobs to burn in the stove. Since the cobs were in the pig yard, gathering them was a very messy job.

Mom's pride and joy was her large flock of chickens, and we loved to find those first little pullet eggs. We sold eggs and young roosters to people from as far away as the Twin Cities, and we had to help dress any poultry sold for food. We hated that job, but the sale of those eggs and roosters put me through college.

When I was 11 years old, Mom promised me a baby sister, and when she arrived I was a regular little mommy, and I loved it.   I also helped with little brother Jim.

With the morning's work done, the afternoon was fun time. Did you ever make mud pies with real eggs? We did, but I don't believe Mom ever knew about it. Our playhouse, under a grove of trees, was behind the hen house so it was very easy to sneak over there and snitch a few eggs. We spent many hours out there. It was nothing fancy--just a clear area with wooden boxes and old discarded pots, pans and dishes. My brother Bill kept his trucks near there, and he was always in the road business. Later our playhouse was moved to a room in an old granary.

My folks loved to go to auctions, and they always came home with boxes of books. That's how we became great readers. One time they brought home a beautiful oak children's table and chairs. In the summer they put the table in our large attic, and we spent hours playing school, and I was always the teacher.

Mom was a great paper hanger, and she had a huge book of wallpaper samples. We girls loved paper dolls, so we made their clothes from wallpaper. In winter, we brought the little table and chairs down to the living room near the pot-belly stove, and my sisters and I had many tea parties. My sister Beverly and I got a tea set for Christmas in the early 40s, and 60 years later I gave it to my daughter Renee for her fiftieth birthday.

The last farm we lived in was southeast of Lismore. It had a huge barn, where we spent many hours playing. It had a large ledge beneath the hay door from which we could jump down into the hay. My sisters Bev, Doree, and I would put on what we believed were wonderful variety shows for little sister Toots and baby brother Jim. I don't know how good those shows were, but I know we scared away a lot of pigeons.

We spent many hours walking the roadside ditches looking for wildflowers. Our farm had two good sized creeks, and we would wade in the water, never thinking how deep it might be. We did some fishing, always hoping Mom would cook the little fish we brought home.

There were lots of neighbor kids to go back and forth with, ponies to ride, and bicycles. Halloween was another fun time. The two neighbor girls would come over, and we would cut out pumpkins. Mom would bake us cookies and make cocoa, and we would take it all out to the pasture line, sit in the dark, talk and enjoy our goodies.

Saturday night was a reward for all our hard work. We drove to Adrian, where the folks shopped and visited and the kids went to the movies-- always westerns. I don't remember if it was a nickel or a dime we were given to spend, but we could get five pieces of candy for a penny, and we guarded that candy with our lives till the next Saturday.

During World War II there were times when we got to go to the show on Sunday afternoons because the folks went to visit our grandparents, Ben and Anna DeLong. We usually came home crying because the movies were about war, and we knew families whose sons were soldiers. After the war, when I was away at college and all the soldiers' families were adjusting to reunion or ultimate loss of their boys, my sister Beverly died in a tragic tractor accident. I still miss her.

I have lots of memories, sad and happy. My folks, by their example and hard work, were very good teachers, and I still practice many of their lessons in my every day life.

Bonnie Broesder Hauser worked as an instructor at Samuel's Beauty School in Sioux City, Iowa. She and her husband Ruben have lived in Iowa City since 1962. They have two adult children and a grandson.

The Broesder family on the farm, 1947: Jim and Toots in front, Dorie and Mom in the middle, Bonnie and Dad in back

A Lesson Learned From Chickens
by Tom Veblen

My mother's drive to make things work went well beyond household chores, lawn and garden tending, and community activities. She couldn't look out the window, it seemed, without thinking up a business scheme. She was, at heart, an entrepreneur.

During that same period, Mother steered me into some money-making ventures, the first of which, selling polliwogs and goldfish to local fish pond owners, turned out to be a clear winner. My mother reasoned that there was always room for at least one more uniquely patterned goldfish in a backyard pond and that polliwogs, the intermediate form of frogs, vociferous eaters of mosquito larvae, would be a sure fire hit with gardeners trying to control their garden's mosquito population.

She was right, and at a nickel for polliwogs and a dime for goldfish, I could sell every one I could get my hands on. The salient feature of this enterprise was its margin of return–100%. The polliwogs and fish were free, the former netted out of Costin's coulee, and the goldfish raised in our basement over the winter, using my mother's adult fish as brood stock.

The resulting revenue all went to the bottom line–nothing but pure profit. Pure magic was more like it. Overnight I was a fully functioning entrepreneur, suddenly able to indulge my material desires, which ran mostly to Saturday afternoon matinees, comic books, and .22 rifle ammunition, while saving for that proverbial rainy day–and college.

My mother's next idea was vegetables. She turned a fair piece of the garden over to my care and helped me select and order the right seeds. Unfortunately every Hallock child's mother had the same idea that year, and when the time came to harvest my beets, beans, peas, carrots, corn, tomatoes, and lettuce, I couldn't give the stuff away. Worse, my mother couldn't stand to see the stuff go to waste so she put me to work helping her preserve it all

And then came her really, really big idea. It seems she had been talking with the county agent, an experienced poultry man, and the two of them had decided that raising chickens would make a great 4H project. Under their tutelage my Boy Scout friends and I would raise chickens. Mother would provide strategic counsel, the county agent would provide direct supervision, and my friends and I would execute the plans. In the process we would learn how to raise chickens, come to know business, earn merit badges, and best of all, get rich!

The scheme sounded good to me, and in a burst of enthusiasm I approached our block-away neighbors, the Bergs, about renting their unused chicken coop. They had tired of chickens (which should probably have given me pause, had I been thinking harder about the matter) and were more than pleased to let me use it. It was an ideal coop, fully equipped with heaters, waterers, feeders, and a fenced run that would easily accommodate my planned 100-bird flock.

With all systems go, the county agent arranged for the purchase of the day-old chicks I would need. He predicted that 6% of the order would die in transit and counseled that I buy 106 to assure the 100 chicken flock intended. He was right on the money. Two weeks or so later, at the crack of dawn, we met the Great Northern's two-car mail delivery train, affectionately known as "the dinky," to receive my peeping, perforated cardboard boxes containing 100 live, three-day-old chicks–and six dead ones. Yuk!

The first several weeks were something of a trial. The little peepers looked too small to survive, and I was certain they would croak and wipe out my entire savings. I spent most of those first weeks hunched over in a corner of the coop waiting for the inevitable. But to my surprise they prospered, and as they grew and could be switched from starter mash to rolled corn and buttermilk, I gradually cut back my constant vigil from eight to six visits each day and then to three.

Based on information gleaned from the 4H chicken-raising manual, and from talking with my experienced chicken-raiser supervisor and others, I knew that it would take 120 days to raise my chicks to fryers ready for market. Given this, my profit from the operation would be somewhere between 75 cents and $1 a bird. Imagine that–a sure $75 or more--a small fortune that would easily cover the purchase of a new bike, new CCM skates, and a new Remington .22 rifle!

My calculations on time and weight proved to be about right. By mid September my 100 peeping chicks were fryers, ready for slaughter. I put my parents on notice that the next Saturday was the day because they had agreed to help me with dressing the birds.

So much for good intentions. What I hadn't counted on was that in the four months of raising those suckers, I had come to know each one of them individually. And they knew me. Three times a day for four months I had visited them, and each time, when I opened the coop door, they would flock about, clucking and scratching, obviously overjoyed with my presence, not to mention my magical feeder-filling powers. Not only that, I reciprocated their obvious affection; they had become my friends.

I decided to put off their execution–just for one week. And then another. September gave way to October. Week by week the birds continued to eat and grow, gradually transforming themselves from fryers into roasters. Ignoring my father's increasingly pointed questions, I continued to put off the grim chore. Then my mother weighed in–and my 4H supervisor. I just couldn't do it.

By the Saturday before Thanksgiving you could cut the tension with a knife. Before dawn that morning my father, obviously decided, shook me awake. "Tom," he said, "today we kill chickens."

And so we did. Setting a chopping block in the doorway of the coop, we proceeded to chop off their heads, one by one. All 100 of them. My friends. One by one, their heads chopped off, we tossed them, blood spurting from their necks, into the snowy yard, there to flap out their lives.

Then, grasping my friends' dead carcasses by their feet, we carried them down into the basement where, one by one we dipped them into a vat of boiling water.

Having stripped their feathers, we then gutted them, wrapping my now naked friends in waxed paper for freezing. It took most of the day, but by the time we were finished–wheezing from inhaling the acrid steam, bone tired and splattered with blood–I had mastered the art of chicken killing and butchering. There I stood at the end of the day, a groggy, dead broke, sadder-but-wiser chicken killer.

It isn't often that one ends a day of work covered from head to foot with the blood of one's friends. It gets one to thinking. And what I thought that day was that I'd never again wait for my father or anyone else to make the decisions I should make for myself. Whether it's chickens to be slaughtered, a marriage gone south, a child gone to drugs, a friend gone to alcohol, or a business deal or investment gone sour (all subsequently real situations), I'd face the music.

It's human nature to put things off until tomorrow, or next Saturday, or next month. But finally, whether you're ready or not, the time comes when the problem must be faced. And when it does, either you make the decision or someone else will make it for you. You can be submissive or sovereign; it is up to you.

The chicken killing lesson? Be sovereign. Take responsibility. Be accountable.

And choose your friends carefully

Hallock native Tom Veblen is a retired general management consultant living in Washington, D.C. with his wife Linda. He has five adult children and enjoys writing, wilderness canoeing, civic activities and traveling.

Farming from the Seat of a Wheelchair
by Arvin Rolfs

How does a 34 year-old farmer from southwestern Minnesota provide for his wife, his three young children, and his widowed mother after being stricken by polio and confined to a wheelchair for the rest of his life? He does what he's always done--he keeps on farming.

This was what confronted Eldra Claussen and his family from Hardwick in 1949 after Eldra was hospitalized for over eleven months in Minneapolis, fighting the disease and trying to recover from its aftermath. But he was not Rock county's only polio victim.

By the end of 1948, when Minnesota recorded 800 cases, Rock County, with a population of a little over 11,000, was reported to have the highest incidence of polio per capita in the nation with 61 cases and 14 deaths.

Although poliomyelitis was commonly referred to as "infantile paralysis," it was not only children who contracted the disease. Of those 61 with a clinical diagnosis of polio, 11 were over the age of 18, and of those 14 who died from the disease that summer, five were adults.

On August 31, 1948, Eldra was rushed by ambulance to the University of Minnesota Hospitals where he joined me, his nephew, who had arrived a week earlier in the polio isolation unit. John Krogmann of Luverne, who joined the family by marrying Eldra's niece Imogene Lemke on the day Eldra was taken to the hospital, spent two weeks of his honeymoon in the polio isolation unit of a Sioux Falls hospital.

After two weeks of isolation from everyone but gowned and masked medical attendants, when the disease was no longer considered contagious, Uncle Eldra and I were split up. He was sent to the Sheltering Arms Hospital in Minneapolis for further recovery and rehabilitation, and I was sent to the Sister Kenny Institute. That was the last we saw of each other until the following August when we were both discharged, primarily to make room for the seasonal influx of new polio patients.

The dream of most hospital patients is to be sent home, the sooner the better, but when physical impairments are involved, home is often where the greatest challenges are faced. In my case it was a simple matter of learning to be a 10-year-old kid again. But in Eldra's case, it was a matter of establishing himself again as the head of his household, the breadwinner of the family and the one who managed the farm affairs.

Communication between Hardwick and Minneapolis in the late 1940s was slow and tedious by mail, and the telephone was inconvenient and pricey for farm folks, so Eldra was largely out of the loop of daily farming decisions until those two hours on Sundays when he and his wife Eunice could visit and talk about issues. The daily decision maker for the most part was my grandfather, Eldra's father-in-law, Leonard Arp, who tried to abide by Eldra's decisions whenever possible. There were times, however, when he had to make some decisions unilaterally.

My grandfather Arp, county chairman of the Agriculture Stabilization Committee for the U.S. Department of Agriculture, was adept at making decisions, and he knew how to take charge. That was good in Eldra's absence, but less good after Eldra returned home. It took only one incident, however, for Eldra to reestablish the proper chain of command. He and Eunice returned from a trip to town one day shortly after his discharge to find a local trucker, under orders from Grandpa, loading up some of Eldra's hogs to take to Sioux Falls for market. Eldra let the sale go through because they were ready for market anyway, but he also asked Grandpa not to do that again. My grandfather bowed out as their decision-maker, but not out of his involvement in their welfare.

At the time of Eldra's hospitalization, the community rallied as it always does for a rural family in distress with the neighboring farmers all pitching-in for the corn harvest of 1948. After the huge event was completed, however, the community went back to its routine, and the family was expected to deal with any leftover challenges on its own. Eunice and the boys, LeeAllen, age 8, and Billy, age 6, managed to take care of feeding and watering the livestock and chickens, milking the cows, and gathering eggs. Grandma Claussen, who lived with the family, cared for baby Marlee and helped with meals. Managing the continuing needs of the livestock and chickens, however, as well as preparing the ground for spring planting, cultivating the crop throughout the summer, and finally harvesting it in the fall were totally beyond Eunice's resources at that point. And that's when friends and family came in.

Immediate neighbors, Wayne Bryan, Paul Groth, Lawrence Hawes, and Walter Moeller, helped however they could, but it was Eldra's brothers-in-law who consistently did what needed doing in those intervening years until Eldra could take an active role in the field work himself and the boys would grow to be able participants. Loryn Arp, Robert Erickson and Herb Lemke of Hardwick, Alvin Boomgaarden of Magnolia, and Walter Rolfs of Kenneth all came to consider Eldra's farming needs as having equal priority with their own.

After his return home, however, Eldra decided it was more appropriate to secure a hired hand than to expect his brothers-in-law to do double duty on a long-term basis. That winter he hired Otto as a live-in hired man to relieve Eunice of her daily outdoor chores, to keep the livestock well bedded and the buildings in repair, and to prepare the machinery for spring field-work. As spring came, however, Otto's previous employer realized his loss in Otto's absence and made him an offer he could not refuse. So Eldra was back to depending on Eunice and their young sons for daily farm duties and on family and friend volunteers for the necessary field work.

To alleviate the stress as best he could, Eldra arranged to have an electric starter and a hand clutch installed on his Farmall tractor and his tractor seat modified so the back-rest could be easily removed and put back in place again. Then he prevailed upon his father-in-law to help him get a ramp built that would enable someone to push him up to tractor level, where he could transfer from the wheelchair to the tractor seat. From that point onward he could be a real farmer again!

My grandfather was reluctant to have Eldra attempt that. He was concerned about real opportunities for injury under those circumstances, but Eldra was determined. So Grandpa designed the ramp, Uncle Loryn built it, and Eldra used it to its full advantage.

By this time the boys were participating more in the heavy labor of farm work, adding to their weekend crew their cousin, Ardean Ladd, Eldra's sister Viola's son. Raising cattle, hogs, and chickens creates a persistent need to clean barns on a regular basis, and this duty fell to the boys every Saturday. To avoid tractor contention at field-work time though, Eldra bought a John Deere for the boys' Saturday specials, reserving the Farmall for his own use.

Boys, left to themselves, are quite able to manage their own ways of getting a job done, and LeeAllen, Ardean and Billy were no exceptions. Perceiving driving the tractor and spreader out to the field to unload its booty as the glory part of the job, they all agreed to take equal turns at it. However, when the senior members of the crew realized that Billy (age 11 by then) was unable to get the tractor into 4th gear for cruising speed and was content with 2nd gear, they judged him to be taking too much time for the trip and compelled him to lose his turn every-other time around.

Our two families were always close, since Eunice and my mother Norma were sisters, but I never did hear much about those labor disputes or any other sibling rivalry squabbles that are bound to occur when brothers work together. But since Eldra and I had both survived polio, our families became even closer, and my brothers and I were very close to LeeAllen and Billy.

My family visited the Claussen family frequently, many times unannounced, and I was impressed by how often they already were entertaining other guests for the evening, sometimes extended family members, sometimes friends. Often it would simply be the man of a neighboring family, seated at the kitchen table playing buck euchre with Eldra and the boys. In the days before TV, the Claussens did not lack company.

My father in particular found Eldra to be compatible as the three of us for several years made our weekly excursions, trying one alternative medical treatment or another in hopes of remedying our impairments. I remember at the time of my discharge from the Sister Kenny Institute how the therapist specifically advised my parents against seeking chiropractic treatment for me. Yet, within a week of my homecoming, Dad was taking me to Doc James in Luverne for treatment. His prescription was two-fold: a glass of grape juice per day and a neck adjustment twice a week. I liked the grape juice part!

Eldra was taking treatments once a week from an osteopath, Dr. Eiselt, in Flandreau, South Dakota. With the doctor's office on a second floor level, it took four men to carry Eldra and his wheelchair up that long flight of steps. While my father occasionally was a part of that four-man team, there was never enough room to include me in the car. But after Dr. Eiselt moved his offices to another building with a street-level entrance, Dad was quick to decide that I should also start taking treatments from Dr. Eiselt. Since Dad was able to manage Eldra in his wheelchair by himself, there was no longer a need for a four-man crew, and that made room in the car for me. Any time I could trade getting my neck cracked twice a week for getting it cracked once a week I was content.

Dad took Eldra and me to see Dr. Eiselt for perhaps a year with no appreciable change in the condition of either of us. By then the family was hearing reports through the grapevine of fabulous results of a touch-doctor in Marion, South Dakota. Eldra and I had only three sessions with him though, until he readily confessed there was nothing he could do for either of us. That was good news for me because I was finding his touches quite traumatizing.

Switching our treatments to Dr. Quinell on the west side of Sioux Falls benefited us all in two ways: it reduced our round-trip excursion from five hours to more like three hours, and Eldra and I both agreed that Dr. Quinell's treatment rooms smelled a lot better! Although I sensed no benefit from his light massages with those sweet-smelling creams nor from the tickle of his electric-shock treatment, Eldra did confide to Eunice that he was beginning to feel better circulation in his feet. By that time, however, my typical half-days of schooling were coming to an end, and the realization by both families was dawning that our search for some kind of treatment to erase the aftermath of polio was futile.

I think we were all disappointed that our quest was over. Dad and Eldra appreciated the benefits those trips afforded them: the pleasure of each other's company, a break from routine, and the opportunity to interact with new people. I was content just to sit in the back seat of the car and listen to Dad and Eldra's conversations and enjoy the hamburger and malt Dad treated me to after each treatment.

Eldra's obstructions to enjoying any quality of life were formidable, yet his demeanor and that of his family belied any frustration or disappointment. Aside from the wheelchair, Eldra was no different from any of my uncles. He interacted in family events as they did, was every bit the card player they were, took part in family picnics, and relished going fishing.

Going to the movies was thwarted by unbending fire-marshal rules (or by theater managers' interpretation of them) that forbade wheelchairs set in the aisles. Drive-in movies in Luverne and Pipestone, and Hardwick's Wednesday shopping-night and free outdoor movie extravaganzas gave Eldra and his family those summertime outlets, which they fully enjoyed.

The long winter days were the hardest on Eldra, though, when all he could do was dream about spring and being on his tractor again. He would occasionally voice the idea of looking into the possibility of small electrical appliance repair, but he had no such training nor any opportunity to receive any. Job retraining programs in rural Minnesota were virtually non-existent, and the Minnesota Department of Vocational Rehabilitation of the 1950s required family relocation to participate in their programs. Reality told Eldra and Eunice to stick with what they knew and with whom they knew.

Recalling my observations of Eldra's attitude shortly after we were released from the hospital and were able to share family events again, now leads me to speculate whether or not small appliance repair really would have been the family-supporting venture for Eldra that he may have dreamed of. Part of his occupational therapy at Sheltering Arms hospital had been to build table lamps out of heavy glass-block ashtrays. In his early months at home Eldra had many requests from friends and family members to build them one or more of those attractive and durable table lamps.

Far from capitalizing however, Eldra charged them only the cost of components, but nothing for his time, effort, and cost of his tools. He had no inclination to profit from what he may possibly have interpreted as their charitable requests. I have no way of knowing how Eldra would have fared in such a business venture. I do know, though, that farming was the business he loved.

At the age of 53, Eldra died doing what he loved, farming as best he could. He died of a heart attack while driving his tractor, pulling a corn chopper and wagon. He managed to stay on the tractor through it all though, until LeeAllen was able to intervene, halt the tractor, and pull Eldra's body to safety.

As Eldra lived in dignity, carrying an indescribable burden without complaint, he also died in dignity, leaving family and friends a worthy memory of Eldra Claussen, a man of honor and courage.

Arvin Rolfs grew up in Rock County, survived polio, taught German, Spanish & English at Bird Island High School for 4 years and currently is a systems analyst, nearing retirement at AgriBank in St. Paul.

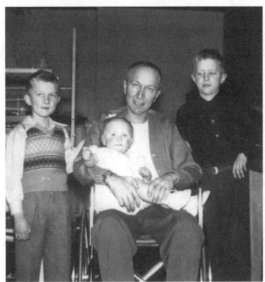

Billy, Eldra & Marlee, and LeeAllen Claussen
at the Sheltering Arms Hospital in Minneapolis, 1949

Next Time, Don't Bring the Kids!
by Kathy A. Megyeri

Every Minnesota family who could afford one or who had inherited one loved his cabin on the lake. Some, like my mother and father who owned a tiny lake cabin, dreaded calls from friends and relatives requesting visitation rights, especially if they toted along kids and pets. Dad worked hard on our weekend retreat, one that our family seldom used because Dad worked all the time. Dad painted, trimmed, mowed, replaced screens, fixed leaks and cleaned gutters, and we never rented out our little primitive wood cabin on Waseca's muddy little lake. Although I was young, I vividly recall two days' worth of visitors that prompted Dad to sell, and sixty years later, his advice to others is to never disclose ownership of a lake front cabin.

He usually discouraged weekend visitors because of its small size, but one weekend in August in the early '50s, Dad relented when an Air Force buddy and family wanted to visit. Mom cooked, cleaned and changed bed linens after receiving a postcard warning of the family's impending arrival. Dad remained in Owatonna for business, but he promised he would join us for the weekend if the family stayed that long, a magnanimous offer.

The family of four arrived, unpacked, and settled in after a quick run to the water to see if there were undertows and tidal waves that were missing from their elegant home on Lake Minnetonka. The older urchin, 9 year-old John, complained that the cabin had no games worth playing. Our Old Maid card game and an Uncle Wiggly board game bored him silly.

Any reminiscing with Mom about old times and the couples' years together in the Air Force based at Truax Field in Madison, Wisconsin was useless because Mark and John whined, complained, cried, and whimpered to their parents about how there was nothing to do in the cabin. The kids wanted ice cream, Cokes, and brownies for their before-bed snacks. Because of a storm, the whimpers for "Mommy" didn't quit until the parents cradled the young-uns in bed between them.

That night, it rained unmercifully; it thundered and lightninged so fiercely that 3-year-old Mark shrieked and cried hysterically for "Mommy, Mommy!" The next morning, cold, windy Canadian air blasted our little cabin on the lake. The "front was coming through," the weatherman said, and our guests apologized for Mark's wetting the bed. Mom started breakfast before laundering bed linens.

Amid 140-decibel screams of "I want orange juice, eggs over-easy, oatmeal, dark toast, Canadian bacon, and Hills Brothers Coffee for breakfast," the already harried hostess (Mom) served a more common fare amid fourteen glasses (the kids took a new one each time they drank) and differing requests from each family member, most left unfilled. No one sat at the table in any semblance of order. Mark took his buttered toast to Mom's newly reupholstered couch. John ate in front of the minuscule black and white Motorola TV, and the parents asked each youngster whether his morning bowel movement was "soft" or "hard." They begged both little tigers to take their vitamins and then discussed entertainment options. The ignored hostess (Mom) was left to wash dishes, make beds and launder sheets in her wringer washing machine.

Moving the guests from the cabin to their Ford Fairlane convertible was not a short, simple task. An hour and a half later, the family and I (as tour guide) motored under raindrops to the little town of Waseca, but the kids spotted a miniature golf course next to town that was open in spite of the rain. While the parents browsed in shops, I was dragged onto the three-hole concrete fairway so Mark could roll the ball through the course with his hands. John threatened to club his little brother at each of the three tees. The game lasted interminably while I kept score and repeatedly explained to the two old geezers sitting on the park bench watching this scene that the kids weren't related to me.

When the golf game finally ended (87 and 26 over par), we became what every Waseca merchant hoped for–rainy day shoppers. I retreated to the bench next to the geezers, claiming I was tired. Two and a half hours later, the four tourists emerged with t-shirts and hats that advertised a Minnesota gopher, a walleyed pike, and an outdoor privy. Somehow, lavender palm trees sprouting from yellow sand appliquéd on one sweatshirt didn't seem quite accurate for Waseca, but I said nothing. "Anything for the kids," the dad explained. The whole shopping expedition confused me because I knew Lake Minnetonka was only 1 1/2 hours away and surely, they had better t-shirts and souvenirs there, I thought.

The weather was still misting so by now, movie lines at Waseca's one theater snaked around the block, and this crew was too hungry to join them. I explained that Mom was cooking and baking enough for all back at the cabin, but they preferred burgers and fries that could be inhaled from paper cups and napkins, so what the heck? Even I opted for a barbecue and a Pepsi at the drugstore counter.

It was close to sundown, but all agreed that if we bundled up, we could walk around the lake before it got dark. But with French fries, ice cream, and pizza sold at an A & W Root Beer stand on the way home, the junk food connoisseurs quickly lost interest in walking. Someone suggested they go back to the town's drug store where they found more t-shirts and caps, except that the dad wanted one with the dancing bear that advertised Hamm's Beer, and all the sweatshirts had hoods. "Who ever wears the hood?" he queried. Mark was tired because he'd had no nap, and he fussed and screamed until his mom quieted him with promises of a treat. He shouted with glee when his dad purchased him a slinky that he stretched from one of the car's fenders to the other so it never returned to its original shape.

That night, John claimed he was sick to his stomach and sure enough, we all watched the departure of the day's intake of junk food. At 2:46 a.m., he suffered an asthma attack, and his parents half-slept sitting up with John between them. We all listened to heaving and wheezing until the dad found an open drug store back in Waseca early the next morning to purchase an inhaler.

Not caring what the breakfast order was, Mom made pancakes for everyone. Her role as hostess had deteriorated to nurse/housekeeper/cook/laundress, grocery shopper/cleaning woman. There was never time quiet enough to talk or share memories. Mark repeatedly dropped his pants to play with his penis. John begged my mother for some stones she'd collected and displayed from the North Shore Drive.

Then John told us his dad was going to buy him a car, a pony, a Roy Rogers cowboy outfit, and recounted for the umpteenth time the story of his stepping on a nail last summer. In retaliation, my mild-mannered mother finally screamed, "Be quiet so I can hear your parents for once!" But then she realized she'd made a reprehensible mistake in reprimanding another's child. I tried to help her over her embarrassment by insisting we all go down to the water before sunset.

An hour after shoes were put on, bathing suits found and pail and shovel retrieved from the car trunk, we all sat at the water's edge. The asthmatic built a fort out of twigs and limbs brought to the water front. He sought approval after every hand pat or effort to increase the size of the fort. While the infant nudist flashed nearby geriatrics who were fishing at the water's edge, his parents slept soundly in the hot sun.

Hours later, welcome word finally came from the sun-fried dad. "Kids, I think we have to get going if we're going to see any more of southern Minnesota." Screams and shrieks of protest followed. The fort wasn't finished, and the streaker hadn't covered the entire waterfront. The adults begged, threatened, cajoled, and praised both boys for good behavior and promised a return to our lake someday soon.

Two hours later, they showered outdoors, a necessity at any lake cabin, but a novelty for them in family togetherness as all four crowded into the outdoor, wooden shower stall simultaneously, much to the horror of my proper and modest mother.

They packed and loaded their car and added Mother and me because we were all on our way to dinner as a goodwill offering to Mom for tolerating sleeplessness and two days' extra work, irritation, and noise. Fortunately, we were seated quickly at the local restaurant, but after we ordered the house specialty, Mark threw butter at the 5-year-old in back of us. I was sure the fathers would battle it out in the parking lot, but it was easier for Mark's dad to pretend he'd seen nothing.

John dumped his tartar sauce under the table, Mark pushed the high chair over and demanded to sit in a "chair just like Daddy's," and Mark highlighted his act by imitating two deaf adults at the next booth who were signing to one another. My mother avoided the disgusting looks from other patrons by dissecting her broccoli and whispering to me that working mothers disciplined less. "They just get too tired, even on vacation."

The father threatened that this would be the last restaurant meal ever if the boys couldn't behave, a threat they'd obviously heard before. The foursome left to use the bathroom after the dad paid the bill, and then it was the waitress's turn to clean up after a family that management claims is always welcome. I overheard my mother whisper to her an apology, "They're not mine."

The loaded car-full drove Mom and me home, and we waved a grateful farewell, even blew a kiss. We were exhausted but ecstatic they were to be someone else's burden tomorrow as they drove across the state visiting their friends with lake-front cottages. We gazed lovingly at the sign I helped Mom hang outside our front door, a sign that may not prevent house guests from coming, but certainly limited their stay:

"Fish and visitors smell after three days."

Mom insisted that we get rid of the cabin we weren't using very often, and the little place on Waseca Lake was sold the next year. No one really missed it that much.

Owatonna native Kathy Megyeri is a retired teacher, a writer, and an educational consultant. She and her husband Les live in Washington, D.C.

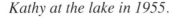

Kathy at the lake in 1955.

The Hat Came Back
by Natalie Battis

In the first four years of my life my family and I lived on a cul-de-sac in Eagan. My mom ran a child care in our house so there was always something to do. There were two boys my age I always played with, and we played some interesting things. One of them ate worms with me in the spring, and they both played in the big pile of snow with me in the winter.

Every winter the snow plow would push all the snow into the middle of the cul-de-sac, and when the snow pile got really high we would put on all of our winter clothes, take out our sleds, climb up the big pile of snow and slide down. Sometimes we built a tunnel that went from one side of the pile to the other.

One tragic day when I was 3 years old, I lost my favorite cow print hat with black spots and a white puff ball on the top. I had been climbing through the tunnel, and I didn't realize my hat was gone until I was inside and my mom asked where I put it. We searched and searched, and when we couldn't find it, I thought I would never see that hat again.

My mom said, "When the snow melts away you will get your hat back." So I started looking forward to the day I would get my hat back, or the day the snow would melt away.

Since we still went outside every day, I had to use a different hat, and I tried not to think about my favorite hat. Then finally the day came when the snow started melting away. Of course the big pile would be the last to melt because there was the most snow in that one spot, and that is where my hat was most likely hidden.

I waited until there was very little snow left, and then I went outside to the big snow pile that was now only half the size it had been. I went out there to get my hat. It took awhile to get out there because I had to put on my jacket, snow pants, and all that stuff to keep bundled up.

I was so happy when I found my cow print hat at the top of the smaller pile that I put it on and ran inside. The only thing I wasn't happy about was that the puff ball that hung from the top had fallen off, so before I ran inside I picked that up too. When I got in the house I took the broken puff ball in my hand, stood in front of my mom and said, "Put it on." So Mom glued the puff ball to the hat.

She did that several times because it snowed again, and the pile of snow got big again, and we kept going outside to play, and the puff ball kept falling off. One day when we were outside in the new tunnel running through the big snow pile, the puff ball came off so I ran over to my mom and said, "The ball came off; the ball came off." When my mom said she would get the glue and glue it back on I said, "No, it's okay now."

I went on without the puff ball, and I wore that hat for many years after. I made sure not to lose it again, and I still have the hat seven years later. The hat does have a glue spot on the top where the puff ball kept getting glued on before we finally left it off. The glue mark on the top of the hat is one reason I remember this story. Of course, the other reason is because I still have the hat, with or without the puff ball on the top. I learned that things like puff balls don't last forever and you just have to deal with that.

Natalie Battis wrote this when she was a fourth grader at Salem Hills Elementary School in Inver Grove Heights, and her teacher, Kathy Gerber, submitted it. Natalie hopes to be a writer when she grows up, and this is her first published piece.

My Red Eversharp
by Father Robert Kieffer

On a warm summer day, a lazy day with only aggravation to occupy me, I went upstairs in the old house and discovered Jim on the bed documenting the rows of popcorn armies he had assembled, or else he was making long columns of numbers on paper. The important thing is that he was using my red Eversharp, the red hard plastic kind.

Being the sort of day it was, he being the sort of person he was, and me the sort I was, I demanded he hand over my Eversharp. Quickly a real battle was waged, a loud and raucous skirmish as we wrestled on the old iron bed. I had his arm over the bedstead and rapped it against the metal brace to make him drop the treasure, but he hung on. The battle reached fever pitch with Jim hollering, "My arm, my arm!" Of course, I was used to his "faking" and was not particularly alarmed. Furthermore, even if he was in pain, it was not so severe that it made him let go, and he was still able to put up a fight.

Suddenly and without warning my mother stood in the doorway. There was trouble. She took the Eversharp and engaged in an old trick of hers. When we would unduly fight over what was whose, she had this frightful practice of breaking whatever it was in two and giving each one half. She tried, but of course, an Eversharp is an Eversharp, hard plastic and steel sleeve. My mother confiscated the pencil. The fight cost me my pencil and my self-righteousness.

Later that evening Jim began lamenting that his arm hurt. I suspected continued fakery. The next day, which was Saturday, he began holding his arm. Sunday morning after church my mother and father took Jim to the hospital. When they came home in the early afternoon Jim was sporting a bright white cast. I had broken his arm, and he had the cast to announce it.

That day my stock had fallen. I remember sitting around the yard not wanting to go into the house. My little brother Tom would come outside at regular intervals to assure me that indeed my stock had truly fallen, and that I would probably have to spend the rest of my life outdoors.

It seemed this lasted for hours. It was late afternoon when Tom passed me his last and latest bulletin; he came to tell me to come into the house. But I wouldn't go in; I stayed sitting on the front step. Then my dad came out and said to me, "Come into the house, tell your brother you're sorry, and that's the end of it." So I did, and I did, and it was. I have never been so relieved. A great load was lifted off me. The Eversharp disappeared. None of us ever saw it again.

The Kieffer kids in the '40s: Diann, Jim, Bobby, Anita

Robert Kieffer grew up in Morris, one of ten children. Anita Poss who wrote "Cowpie" is his sister. He was ordained a Catholic priest in 1969 and is pastor of Our Lady of Victory Church in Fergus Falls.

Helga and Me
by Father Robert Kieffer

A Saturday Christmas is not a good arrangement for a priest; an interlude of two or three days before the weekend is better. But Den and Bev invited me to Alexandria for Christmas dinner, and their kids and grandkids would be there. The truth is, Christmas without company isn't a holiday, unless, of course, you're sick or something dreadful has happened. Barring all of these, on Christmas morning after the 10:30 mass I drove to Alexandria. With a brandy Manhattan in one hand and shrimp hors d'oeuvres in the other, I settled into a full afternoon of smart talk and gracious living, careful to be moderate so to drive safely home.

We had a festive time, and then we were to open presents, which I was not counting on. I was going to sit this one out in the adjoining room, but they wouldn't have it! So we crowded together, the wrapping paper, the twelve of us, the ribbons, the bows, the treasures in the boxes. It was fun, and I was in a good mood.

Then it was time to go home. It was Saturday; could Sunday be far behind? I was making my farewell gestures, but there was one more gift. "Wait, wait a minute!" In came a carrier, a cat inside called Madeleine, and food, a dish, and a depository with litter box liners. Stunned doesn't quite capture the mood. I did not say thank you as Bev and Dennis explained they would take Madeleine back at any time, if we didn't become friends. Just so, Madeleine and I drove tenuously home to Fergus Falls.

Into the house and down the basement I positioned the litter box in front of the carrier and then opened the door. Her head came out but the rest stayed in. I let her be. For a week I saw neither hide nor hair, only deposits in the litter box and food disappearing from her dish. She was alive, but my call was only answered by a faint meow. I was thinking she crawled between the wall and the basement foundation, but I have discovered she likes under the furnace and behind the washer. One day at noon I found her upstairs studying herself in the fireplace glass; the next day she was so intent she didn't notice me come in.

From then our relationship developed. I changed her name to Helga Marie when I learned she was a Norwegian Forest Cat. It is a good hollering name, and also seemed appropriate for a priest's cat living among the Scandinavians. Now she sleeps on my feet at night and cuddles with my shoes during the day.

We talk to each other; she seldom meows. She follows me from room to room, and I call her if she demurs as cats are wont to do. She stretches in an inviting way, and I brush her and tickle her belly. Helga was my good gift at the end of the millennium. Today I bought her a fuzzy blanket to keep her cool in the summer and warm in the winter, so the ad read. Helga does not like Whiskas cat food. I might have known; it was four cans for a dollar. We're doing Christmas all year round-- Helga and me!

Helga

Northland Summer of 1939
by Richard Hall

Although more than six decades have passed, when I reflect on the years of the Great Depression, the summer of 1939 stands out as one of the most memorable times in my life. Things were starting to get better, but a lot of able-bodied married men were still looking for any kind of steady work. They would be hired before me--a teenager with no work experience.

When school let out for summer, one kid I hung around with got a job working on a farm for $10 a month, his board, room, laundry and cigarettes. I thought he had it made. Another friend helped his dad, who was a carpenter. Even the youngest tag-along pal got a job working on a mink farm and a paper route, but I couldn't find a job. The Hormel plant in Austin hired a few, but I was too young to apply.

I had about $2 in savings. Without telling anyone, I took my jacket, and with just the clothes on my back I hitchhiked to St. Paul looking for work. I was able to find my way to my grandfather's house.

My grandfather, who was around 60 years old, had managed flour mills and had been foreman in several meat packing plants. All he had was a small house and an old car. In those days there was no Social Security, medical or unemployment insurance or pensions, so my grandfather had very little to show for many years of hard work. Every now and then he was able to find a little part-time work.

His wife, who was about ten years younger, had a steady job in a small hotel working for low wages. They were having a hard time living from day to day. They told me men were looking for jobs everywhere, and there were no steady jobs to be had in St. Paul. I stayed for supper and stayed the night. After breakfast the next morning, I started hitching rides north to my Uncle Ed's cabin near Big Sandy Lake in Aitkin County.

I don't remember how I was able to get all the way to the north edge of St. Paul, but I remember I walked a lot, and it was very hot. An old farmer with a small truck picked me up and gave me a ride to his farm on the highway near Soderville. He was somewhat grumpy, but when I got out of the truck he told me his son had a cabbage farm next door, and I should go see him about a job. I did, and he offered me a job at a dollar a day and board and room.

I was to stay in his old room in his father's farmhouse and eat breakfast and supper there. The boss's wife would bring us our noon lunch. He told me if I wanted to go to work immediately he would even pay me a full day's pay. I took the job.

My job was to sit on a drag behind a team of horses with a large box of cabbage plants on each side while the hired man drove the team. I was to place each cabbage plant in a row so far from the last one without stopping until all the boxes were empty. The drag stirred up dry dirt, and with a slight breeze I was covered with itchy peat soil. Even my glasses were covered so I had to look over their rims to see. At noon the boss's wife came with sandwiches and lemonade, and we went over to the shade of some trees and ate.

We worked until 5 o'clock. When I got back to the father's farmhouse, he gave me a bar of soap and a towel and told me there was a wash pan on a stand near the pump where I could wash up with cold well water. This guy did not have a wife, but he had a daughter somewhat older than me who did all the cooking.

After supper I had nothing to do, and I saw they could use help with their chores so without being told or asked, I helped the farmer and his daughter milk a dozen cows by hand. I had some experience so I did some of the milking, and the daughter would strip them after I got done.

He showed me my room, which was nice and clean with a ceramic pitcher of cold water and a glass on the table and a ceramic pot under the bed. They had a bathroom on the first floor, but I was told to use the outhouse. When I asked about bathing, the farmer told me there was a swimming hole next to an iron bridge less than a mile down the road, and I could take my soap and towel down there. It was dark by the time I got back, and I had no clean clothes.

The next morning the farmer woke me at daybreak and told me I had to help him with his chores for my board and room. I told him my under-standing with his son had been that I was to get a dollar a day and board and room. He said, "Get up. You have to help with chores." The daugh-ter didn't help this time. When I asked the son about his previous day's offer, he said he told me a dollar a day and board and room, but since I was sleeping an eating in his father's house, there was nothing he could do about it.

As much as I needed the money, after three days I'd had enough, and I quit and got my $3. When I returned to the farmhouse, I expected the father to offer me supper, but he didn't. He told me that if I helped him with chores I could eat supper, stay the night, and leave early the next morning after breakfast. I was desperate. In those days there weren't many cars traveling in the evening, and I was tired and hungry.

Since I had worked three days wearing the same clothes, they were so filthy that I figured nobody would want me in their car. My jacket was okay because I hadn't worked in it. I found an old pair of bib overalls in the barn that were much too large, and after chores when the farmer and his daughter were listening to their radio, I took my soap and towel to the swimming hole, took a bath, and washed my clothes. I put on the old overalls and my jacket and went barefooted, carrying my wet clothes and shoes down the gravel road in the dark. I hung my clothes on a fence behind the barn, washed my feet, and got back upstairs while the farmer and his daughter were still listening to their radio.

The next morning my clothes were cold and damp, but I managed to get them on before anyone was moving around. After we got chores done and ate breakfast, I started on my way. My Uncle Ed's place was a hundred miles away, and on a weekday there were hardly any cars going north. The farther I went, the fewer cars I saw. I had to walk a lot. Outside McGregor I was able to get a ride to Sather's store.

From Sather's the trees came up to the edge of a narrow dirt and gravel winding road on both sides, blotting out much of the sky, but since there was no traffic I stayed in the center of the road. Once in awhile I could see an opening in the trees and the moon would light my way. But most of the time it was very dark. Occasionally I could see a dim light from a cabin or hear the bark of a dog.

The only thing I'd eaten since breakfast was a couple of Baby Ruth candy bars I'd gotten in Mora. I needed rest, and I was cold and hungry. About the time I'd decided to lie down and sleep, I saw two headlights coming from behind, and I caught a ride. We went past a bar, and they dropped me off at O'Connor's store, which was closed. I was able to get a drink from the pump before I continued in the dark past a fire tower and school, where I could see the moon.

The trees became thick again, and I couldn't see the moon as I continued down the center of the road in the dark until I came to a wide opening where a swamp or bog came up to the road. On the east side of the road was a community dump. In those days there was no garbage man, and people dumped their trash at places like this. I knew bears liked to look for food at dumps, and I was scared, but there was no other way.   As I hurried down the center of the road I heard a noise and took off running. As I looked back, with the moon shining down, I could see a skunk with its tail in the air running for cover.

I went back down the center of the road in the dark until I came to an opening that was Prairie River, and I could see the moon again lighting my way. I knew that I was close to Uncle Ed's place because I had been here many times. I crossed the road and found a string of a dozen mailboxes. Even in the dark, everything was familiar now. As tall trees blocked out the sky, the only thing to guide me was a dim lamp from Uncle Ed's cabin. I was able to find its door in the dark, and I knocked. My uncle, who wasn't expecting me, didn't know who I was until I told him.

Inside the cozy little cabin, the wood in the cook stove crackled while Aunt Lill fixed me something to eat. After I'd eaten, we huddled around the table with the oil lamp in its center, and Lill brought out pictures of relatives and mutual friends. There were pictures of people with fish caught, and although I was excited about going fishing, I was so tired that I couldn't keep awake. Lill fixed my bed, and I went right to sleep.

The next morning I woke refreshed with a cool breeze and the smell of pine coming through the partly open window above my head. Later Ed made me sit at the table and write my father and grandfather to let them know where I was and that I was safe.

My uncle Ed owed my dad money for his share of my grandmother's funeral expenses so my dad and Uncle Ed made a deal. If I could stay with Ed for the summer, Dad would cancel Ed's debt. Dad knew he'd never get the money anyway, and I loved being in the north country, so it wasn't a bad deal. I would get my board and room and be expected to help Ed with his minnow business.

Ed was the only bait dealer fishermen could depend on to have shiners. He sold them for 25 cents a dozen, and he sold crappie minnows for 15 cents or two dozen for a quarter. I became Ed's helper seining minnows and helping out with customers. From years of experience Ed knew minnow behavior. He would look at the sky, check the wind, and tell me to load up because we were going after minnows. I would go get the minnow net from where we left it drying from our last trip, load it on Ed's flat bed truck, and go get two large cream cans, Ed's rubber boots, and two galvanized pails. If it was dark, Ed would get his flashlight. We would take off down the loose gravel Horseshoe Lake Road to the beaches on the east side of Lake Minnewawa.

Throughout the summer we all got along fine and had many good times, but my fondest memory is of the Fourth of July. Relatives and friends came to the cabin to visit and fish, and for me it was exciting to see so many interesting adults. Carloads of people came from as far as the Cities, parking their cars wherever they wanted. Since many had not seen each other for a year, there was much laughing and shouting. They brought baskets of food, and everyone pitched in to help prepare the feast as the yard and cabin overflowed with friends.

The men caught and cleaned fish, and the women cooked on Lill's stove and on an abandoned stove twenty feet from the cabin. I had to get water from the pump and wood for the stoves, and both of them used an extraordinarily large amount of wood. Out in the open the food tasted delicious, and there was way more than enough.

It was the biggest time of year for the minnow business. As customers tried to find a place to park, I had to try to drop everything else to look after them. Ed invited a few customers to stay, and they came back with more food and cases of beer. People sat at Ed's big picnic table, on the ground, and some even took out the back seats of their cars and set them on the lawn.

That night there was a big dance at the Minnewawa Retreat Pavilion. I was only 16, so my job was to stay home and look after the cabin and take care of minnow customers. After midnight carloads of people, tired from a full day of partying, came back to find a place to spend the night. There must have been more than a dozen trying to sleep in the cabin, but the bed, floor, and Army cots would only sleep eight. I got up at daybreak to take care of minnow customers, and as soon as I was going out the door two who were sleeping on the floor jumped into my bed.

 Outside people were sleeping everywhere--in cars, on the picnic table, in hammocks tied between trees and in a tent pitched in the yard. In time, the women had coffee brewing on both stoves and were making pancakes for the whole gang. A few went fishing after breakfast, the women stayed around the cabin visiting, but by late afternoon everyone had loaded their cars and headed for home. Although that summer of 1939 holds many memories, no day stands out more vividly than the Fourth of July.

Austin native Richard Hall lives in Rochester with his wife Mickie. He has written three books and made hundreds of pen and ink illustrations.

A Jar In Tennessee
by Michael Finley

You know those microcassette recorders, that cost $29? I buy them not quite like candy, but often enough that there are several around the house.

They are great for taking notes when out walking. Sometimes people see you and think you are schizophrenic, talking to your hand, but that is a small price to pay, in my mind, for being able to "write" on the fly.

Okay. Imagine it is a beautiful fall morning, and I am walking my big standard poodle Beauregard at Crosby Farm Nature Area, alongside the Mississippi River in Saint Paul. It is an undeveloped park with lots of paths cutting through trees along the shore--a perfect place for a scofflaw to let his dog run wild for a few minutes.

And I have the microcassette machine in my pocket, a generic blister-pack Sony. The morning is gorgeous, with new fallen leaves ankle-deep, and white vapor rising from the river. A four-point deer pokes his head into a clearing.

My dog begs me to chase him. It's his favorite game, a role reversal because chasing others is the center of his life otherwise. But I'm game, and I chug along for a hundred yards with him. We take several switchbacks, going deeper into the trees. When we arrive at the riverbank, I feel in my pocket for the recorder. It's gone.

You know how when something is gone you check every pocket eleven times to make sure it's gone? Well, this is gone. I figure I either dropped it when I made my last note, or it fell out of my pocket during my little jog. So I begin backtracking. The dog wants me to chase him some more, but my mood is rapidly darkening, and I decline.

Leaves have been falling in large numbers, so the ground is covered with brown shapes and jagged shadows, all of which look like my little machine. I begin calculating in my mind the loss of the unit -- maybe $40.

Besides, they wear out quickly because you are always dropping them and knocking them on table tops. I look everywhere I walked -- about a two-mile distance -- for the little machine. No luck.

I am nearly reconciled to the loss when I spot it, lying on a patch of bare dirt. The battery and tape compartments are both sprung open, and the tape and batteries lay splayed out on the ground, as if a squirrel or crow has given some thought to taking them home, and then said, nah.

I pop the machine back together and push the play button, still ready for the worst, a dead unit. But instead I hear my own voice. I am talking about Sao Paulo Brazil, which I visited on business two weeks before. On the tape, I am sitting in a bus on a smoggy artery heading out of town, talking to myself about the beggars I see crouched by the highway signs, and the advertising, with the nearly naked models, and the infinite pastel rows of high-rise apartment buildings.

And now I am standing in a clearing in the forest, 7000 miles away, hearing my high, speeded-up voice. The woods are so quiet that this little machine and its tinny little speaker ring clear through the air. Nearby birds, hearing my recorded chatter and finding it suspicious, take wing and flap away to a safer roost.

If you have ever stood between two mirrors and seen the illusion of infinite regression in them, you have an idea what I am feeling, addressing myself electronically from a place so different and so far away.

And if that was not stunning enough, I flip the tape over -- I do not want to tape over this interesting travelogue -- and there is my daughter's voice, talking to a caller on the phone. I reuse my answering machine tapes in my hand recorder, and this tape is perhaps five years old, when my little girl was 8. Her voice sounds so clear, so young and lovely. I forgot what she sounded like then. I can't tape this over either.

The dog, meanwhile, is standing there looking at me with that panting grin dogs wear when they are in their element to the hilt. But the look on his face just now is all wonderment and admiration. He understands very little that I do, but this latest trick, picking something up in the woods and having it talk to me in my own voice, well, this just takes the cake.

Insurance company executive/poet Wallace Stevens once wrote a simple poem called "A Jar in Tennessee," which said that placing a human artifact on a hill in Tennessee changes everything about the hill and Tennessee. Consciousness places frames of meaning on the wilderness.

That's what I see in the look in Beau's eye. It's entirely likely, as Stevens is his favorite poet. And it is a gorgeous day, with the scent of sand and pine adrift like microscopic confetti in the morning breeze, and I do enjoy walking.

St. Paul resident Mike Finley has worked as a newspaperman in Worthington, a TV producer for the University, and a columnist for the Saint Paul Pioneer Press. His website is http://mfinley.com.

The Blue Bicycle
by Michael Finley

The woods echoed with the crunch of boots and the snapping of wood. "How much longer?" my 8-year old son asked.

"Not long," I said, huffing frosted steam. "We're almost there."

My 12-year old daughter was impatient, "What are we looking for?"

"Something you'll never see again," I said. I was in heaven, luring my kids out into the cold to reveal a private mystery. We finally came to a clearing overlooking a gully. We just stood there for a moment, our breath frosting up before us. "It's right here," I announced.

There wasn't a sound except the fluffing of heavy falling snow. Then Jon said, "I see it!" He pointed up, into the lower reaches of a cottonwood tree. There, about ten feet from the ground, was a rusted old bicycle. It was not sitting in a branch; rather, the branch had somehow grown around the bicycle. The main bar was enclosed in swarming wood.

"Wow," Daniele said. I had come across it a few days earlier, walking the dog. I had passed that spot a hundred times and not noticed. Who looks up a tree to see a bicycle? It takes luck. It is a blessing.

Based on the style, the corrosion, and the absence of rubber, I guessed the bicycle had been in the tree for over 40 years - about my age. It was entirely rusted except for a narrow path of etched blue enamel just below the handlebars, by the little plate that still said Western Automatic.

The four of us were giddy with the idea of a bicycle growing in a tree. How did it get there? Did someone lean it against the tree years ago, and the tree slowly reached out and lifted it up, an inch a year, up into the sky? Or did someone just throw it up there, and the tree grew around it? Whose bike was it, and would that person remember the bike? Did the bike think it was flying? Did the tree think it was riding a bike? Did the wind once blow the wheels around, whispering tales of locomotion in the ear of the stationary tree?

Everyone agreed, on the way back to the car, it was a wonderful thing, and we should always keep our eyes keen for other anomalies. They must be everywhere, we reasoned. We just have to train ourselves to see them.

But a funny thing happened. The next time I visited the clearing, in spring, by myself, not only was the bicycle gone -- but so was the tree. A big wind blowing up the river has no trouble toppling trees rooted in sand. The cottonwood lay accordingly on its side, head down into the ravine, its roots reaching up like imploring hands.

I looked under the tree for the bicycle. I looked around the area, to no avail. The snow was gone, and this year's vegetation was pushing up from the ground -- just high enough to disguise a jutting pedal or tipped wheel rim.

Over the next couple of years I gently obsessed about finding the bicycle, returning to the spot numerous times to see if I had merely misplaced it in my mind. Occasionally I thought I saw it. But it was just a curl of vine, pretending to be wheel, or the color of rot pretending to be rust. I had already seen the outrageous sight, gotten credit for showing it to my family -- what more did I want?

Yet my heart quickened. A bicycle fashioned of iron from the earth once roamed this city and raced up and down its hills. And now it had returned to the earth. Everything combined to make it so. Every falling leaf covered it up in the fall. Each fresh clump of snow that blanketed it in winter. Each springtime splash of rain, every summer footfall -- buried it deeper in the wood. I am so glad I saw it and showed it to my kids. It is in my heart, forever blue, coasting through the living world.

Ushering at the Passion Pit
by Don Matejcek

After I got my driver's license in the spring of 1959, I needed a job so I could afford to put gas in Mom's car whenever she let me use it. My job search ended when the Owatonna Drive-in Movie opened for the season, and they hired me to be an usher.

Drive-ins were popular summertime hang-outs in small towns and on the outskirts of cities, but as real estate values went up, most of that land was sold to more lucrative, year-round business enterprises. A few are still standing, but a vacant lot next to Owatonna Manufacturing Company on County Road 45 now shows no sign of that drive-in movie theater.

As an usher, I was supposed to direct cars into parking places and help keep traffic moving through the gate. I was also supposed to watch for kids sneaking in after the show started, and help clean the concession stand and bathrooms, and watch for people trying to steal speakers.

When a car full of people pulled into its parking space at the drive-in, the first thing they did was remove the metal speaker from its post and hook it onto the side car window. Each speaker was attached to a cable fastened to a post because cordless electronics hadn't been invented yet. One of the most common maintenance problems at drive-ins was caused by customers who occasionally left with the speaker still attached to their car. A few of these thefts were accidental, but many were intentional. I don't know what people thought they would do with those speakers when they got them home. Maybe they just wanted to use them as room decorations because they weren't good for anything else.

The other big problem for drive-in managers was trying to stop kids from sneaking in. Ticket sellers counted passengers in each car going through the gate, but high school kids typically tried to sneak extra people in by hiding them in the trunk or making them scrunch down on the floor of the back seat. I wasn't very good at catching kids sneaking in. In fact, I sometimes sneaked kids in when I came to work in my mom's car. Another way to sneak in was to climb over the fence.

From outside anybody could see the movie on the screen, but to hear the dialog they'd have to be near one of the speakers attached to posts inside. Fence climbers sometimes joined friends in cars. About a block north of the drive-in there was a manufacturing company, and a few blocks west of that was a migrant camp that each summer filled with workers from the South. One night the head usher, Milan Johns, called me over and said that a bunch of people were climbing over the fence between us and the manufacturing company. We ran over that way to chase them out, and Milan yelled, "Stop! You'll have to leave."

We heard a series of clicks, and we were afraid this might be the sound of switchblade knives opening. We never found out if this was true because Milan yelled, " That's okay. Come on in."

Drive-in managers occasionally had "Buck Night," when a car load could get in for one dollar.   Kids got very creative and crammed as many people as possible into cars and trunks. One kid bought an old mail truck and used that. Of course, once they got inside, they had to figure out a way to comfortably watch and hear the show. With that many people in a car, it wasn't easy.

The movie couldn't start until dark, and in Minnesota it doesn't get dark in the summer until after 9, so in many towns the drive-in was the last business to close at night. Double features ran until 1 or 2 a.m., and sometimes they showed films from dusk till dawn. I woke many people up after the lot cleared and a few remaining cars still sat with their speakers tethered to their windows. Sometimes it was light by the time I got home so Mom let me sleep in.

Since tickets were cheap, drive-in owners tried to make extra money by selling concessions, and during intermission, the concession stand got very busy. A short, musical ad on the screen encouraged customers to buy snacks at the concession stand, and that ad really worked. The stand sold hamburgers, fries, and malts, along with an assortment of candy, pop and popcorn. Of course, some people brought their own snacks, and there was nothing to stop them from doing so. But concessions in those days were reasonably priced, so freshly popped popcorn or a cold drink for a dime were tempting treats on a hot summer night.

Drive-ins were sometimes called passion pits because couples could make out in the privacy of their own cars. But one thing that put a damper on this was the presence of Minnesota's favorite pest--the dreaded mosquito. Closing the car window didn't really cut it on a hot night, and covering yourself with mosquito repellent killed the romance. Some tried burning a scented ring on the dashboard, but that didn't work very well either. To further squelch the passion, we ushers had to act like chaperones once in a while when we came around with flashlights to look into cars.

On slow nights I visited the projection booth and learned a few tricks of the trade. Every movie was between six to eight reels long. A bell would ring, and about fifteen seconds later, up in the right hand corner of the screen, you'd see a little dot appear. This was the signal for the projectionist to light the arc in the other projector to ensure a smooth transition between reels. A short time later another dot would appear, and that was the signal to start the other projector and turn off the first one. This was controlled by a foot switch. If the movie was out of focus or if the film broke, patrons would express their annoyance by honking their horns and flashing their headlights. This was very annoying to the projectionist who was trying to fix the problem

I only earned 75 cents an hour, but I saw movies like *North by Northwest, Ben Hur, Some Like it Hot, Suddenly Last Summer, Anatomy of a Murder, Vertigo, Please Don't Eat the Daisies, The Birds, GI Blues, Butterfield 8, The Magnificent Seven, Spartacus* and *Psycho*. One of my all-time favorites was *Guns of the Timberland* with Alan Ladd. They had all played at the indoor theaters earlier, but a good movie is usually good the second time around.

They still have a few drive-in movies, but they look different now. The posts that held the speakers are gone because soundtracks are transmitted to car radios. Although drive-ins gave us an opportunity to see an old movie for a small price, there is really no need for them now because kids can rent a video to watch at home. I don't think either my kids or my grandkids ever saw one, and I'll bet they don't have a clue about why drive-in movies were such a big deal to us back in 1959 and 1960.

Don Matejcek is a fleet maintenance technician for Owatonna Utilities.

Marsh Hawk
by Betty Vos

We returned to our Minnesota north woods home the morning after Mothers' Day, after laying over a day because of high winds. Grass was still short from winter's hold, but greening from spring rains. Forsythia was the only thing in bloom in the flower beds; tulip leaves were up, but buds were tight and small. Pussytoe heads held sway in patches on the lawn, and marsh marigolds lit the floor of the black ash swamp.

Tuesday morning we walked to the far end of our 40 acres, where long ago the last glacier laid down a rough circle of small boulders. Dew still shimmered on grasses from the cool mid-30s night, but the sun warmed things quickly. Wild strawberries were just opening in the sand pit, where they faced no competition. Tamaracks wore their hazy blue-green beginnings tentatively, uncertain whether to take the next step and leaf out fully. Our path was soft from recent rain but displayed no standing water. And mercifully, there were no bugs.

As we neared the aspen grove, our path was blocked by a large tree brought down in our absence, probably by the same high winds that slowed our travels. We stood a moment trying to discern a path around it but saw none – too recent, perhaps, for deer meanderings to leave evidence of their new route. Could we lift a tree? We placed ourselves on either end and hefted, and it rose easily, a frail skeleton of its former self. We heaved it to one side and wondered if the deer would be grateful humans had restored their landscape.

Only grass and club moss showed green in the circle. I sat for awhile on the southeast stone baking in the welcome sun, then rose to see if the east marsh showed any signs of water. At wood's edge I peered out over the marsh grass and saw none – no place for ducks to splash down this year. I put my foot down carefully on the first hummock and watched the ground slowly moisten in my footprint. The marsh stayed hidden, to be discovered only by those who knew it was there. But the marsh hawk knew. She rose noisily as I took my next step out into the clearing, so swiftly I could not pinpoint where she came from. I was doubly startled, being so used to her silent flight.

She gave a stress call and circled overhead, scolding me-- or perhaps issuing a warning to turn around. I watched a long time before I got her message and backed my way towards the woods. I'm sure she was sitting on a nest, and I had come too close. She wheeled into the distance, and we took her cue and walked back to our home, hoping she'd return to hers.

Spring was on us in a rush. Swallows returned the next day, and by Thursday morning the first tulip had opened, followed that afternoon by a daffodil, and choke cherry was suddenly abundant everywhere we looked. That night we watched in awe as the full moon slowly succumbed to earth's shadow, but went to bed before it started its recovery.

The next morning the bluebirds came back. For the first time in our five years here, there were no battles with the swallows. We finally got it right – birdhouses for the swallows in the yard, and solitary housing for the bluebirds on a post at the west edge of the sand pit. We watched at least two pairs perch on the top line of our fence and drop into our lawn for grubs. Good hunting! We hoped they also ate mosquitoes.

Barely a week later, we discovered a soft carpet of downy feathers at the south end of the lawn, against the fence line. No carcass or tail feathers – just soft reddish down with a blue-gray tip. Another hunter had found bluebird for breakfast. I did not connect the two events until we walked again to the stone circle on Memorial Day. By now the wood anemone and white violets were in full bloom, and the sand pit strawberries had set hard green fruit. We paused in the deer stand, camouflaged from peering eyes, and wondered what we'd see if we stayed there round the clock.

A shaft of sunlight through the slit opening caught the soft blue top of Bob's hat and its reddish beige suede bill. This time the hawk's approach was quiet, and she was nearly on us in a low silent swoop before I gasped and pointed. Bob turned, and she must have seen his motion. We made eye contact, then she wheeled at the last second, flying over us and heading south to her nest. What breakfast would she find this morning?

Bounty for the marsh hawk, if not the bluebird.

Virginia resident Betty Vos is a writer, consultant and editor.

Winona State, 1908
by Marilyn Mikulewicz Baranski

I have always been a pack rat--but a very neat and organized one-- who enjoys old news clippings and old correspondence. Recently I rediscovered a 14-year-old letter from Mildred Thomas Lewis who was 102 years old when she wrote. Mildred had graduated from Winona Normal School and had traveled across the country to teach in Vallejo, California. Sixty years later I graduated from Winona State and moved on to also teach in Vallejo. What were the odds of his coincidence? Mrs. Lewis and I had a lot in common.

Let me share one of the letters I received from Mildred Thomas Lewis. It gave me the flavor of what it was like to be a student at Winona State University almost a hundred years ago when it was called Winona Normal, and it gave me insight into Mrs. Lewis herself.

April 18, 1990

Dear Marilyn,
How nice that you wrote me, and I am sorry that I have been so long in answering. Time has caught up with me, and old age is taking over.

I have fond memories for dear old Winona Normal, and I graduated in June, 1908. Guy Maxwell was president then, and we had just one big building, and it housed every class from kindergarten through high school.

My class was the kindergarten--a two-year course, and tuition was $35 a year. I forget how many girls were in my class. Our lovely teacher was Rebecca Martin.

I had a room in Morey Hall. It had been named after the first college president. My roommate was a girl from Minneapolis who was in my high school class, Mary Wisily. We had a large room my first year, and she took the one-year course. She married Harry Stott, a Winona businessman. She later was killed in an accident.

Morey Hall had been converted from a hospital. My second year room had been the operating room, and was a very nice single room which I really enjoyed.

I loved Winona, and have so many fond memories of dear friends. We belonged to the "horse and buggy" days as there were very few cars then. We had so many pleasures--went canoeing on the lake and Saturday night we went to the dance hall or went roller skating. The dining hall was in Morey Hall--cost was $30 a month for three meals a day.

Where the rumors started that I was teaching at the age of l02, I have no idea. Anyway, 'tisn't so. I am nursing a bad leg, and it will be a long time healing.

Many of my friends in Vallejo are either deceased or have left. Too bad that we didn't know each other while I was in Vallejo as we could have had some fun comparing events of the past. But Hurrah for dear old Winona. Love and best wishes .

Mildred Lewis

I received her letter in 1990, and although we had never met, we had exchanged a few letters. I wanted to know more about the woman who had lived the same life as I had--only 60 years earlier. I was impressed by her solid memory at l02 and wanted to learn more about Mildred Thomas Lewis.

Fortunately, I found her daughter Susan's name in the phone book. Susan repeatedly said how much people loved her mother, and how her warmth brought joy to those around her. She spoke lovingly of her mother and said that she was so popular as a first grade teacher that she was the only married woman who was allowed to teach in the Vallejo district in the early years.   At that time, all women had to resign when they married. Susan considered her mother's exemption from this rule to be quite an honor. She said that when Mildred Lewis tried to retire, parents asked her to continue just a little longer until their children completed first grade. She was immensely popular and had a lot of political influence.

I asked if her mother had any practices that affected her longevity. She said there was no cancer or diabetes in their family. Her mother lived her life as a modern woman. She did smoke for many years, but quit suddenly one day after her grand daughter asked her to stop. Mrs. Lewis also drank alcoholic beverages on social occasions. She was a good cook, but not a gourmet. Her food was always tasty but not fancy, Susan remembered. She loved to go to the movies and adored television.

Mildred Thomas married a Navy commander, stationed at Mare Island during World War II. Justice Lewis commanded his own ship and had seen action shooting down Japanese planes. Susan said that other men liked Mildred, but she couldn't be bothered with any of them. She had her class and her family, and they were all she needed.

Susan remembered a time when her mother was driving their circa 1925 Chevy sedan with the little shades on the windows. A bearing suddenly burned out, and the first thing out of Mildred Lewis's mouth was, "Don't tell your father!" Modern woman or not, she was not going to take a chance of losing her driving privileges because she broke the family car.

On another occasion Mildred was driving her two young daughters and her mother back from an outing in Napa. Suddenly a motorcycle officer pulled her over and said, "Lady you are a menace on this highway."

"Why, whatever did I do? " she asked.

"You are going too slow! That is what you did." the officer sneered.

I can look back to almost a hundred years ago and imagine the pretty red-haired Mildred canoeing on Lake Winona. Morey Hall, where Mildred lived, was still used as a dorm when I attended Winona State sixty years later. The dorm adjoined Shepard Hall, where I lived, and I remember going down to study in the quiet and otherwise deserted basement of Morey Hall in what at one time had been a dining room. Remnants of old food serving equipment were still stored there, and I heard stories that in times gone by dormitory supervisors very strictly gave young women etiquette lessons there while they ate their meals.

We had never heard that Morey had once been a hospital. I couldn't imagine where the old operating room had been, but some of my friends swore that ghosts roamed the halls. At the time I just thought that the stories were from teenage girls needing a little excitement. Now though, I wondered if the so-called ghosts were patients who had met a painful demise within those walls, as medical treatment was pretty primitive in those days, and pain medication was limited.

I researched a bit further and discovered that the Morey that Mildred Lewis referred to was an older building on Broadway. The newer Morey Hall, built with a similar design to the old converted hospital, was built in 1911. Maybe the ghosts from the old place came to check out the newer Morey Hall.

How can this pack rat be faulted for keeping such a treasure as a hand written letter from one of the early graduates of my alma mater? Although we never met, I feel somehow connected to her through her letters. Mildred Thomas Lewis died just shy of her 104th birthday. Through her life, I think she made Winona State proud, and I feel proud to have shared a bit of her history.

Marilyn Mikulewicz Baranski graduated from Winona State and taught in Vallejo, California until her retirement in 2003, She and her husband Fred have an adult daughter.

118

My Brother Mark
by Marilyn Mikulewicz Baranski

This was difficult to write because although I have thought of it daily, it has been too painful to really allow my mind to explore this tragic event that forever changed my family. I awakened thoughts and visions that have remained asleep in my mind all these many years.

We were a normal farm family in Dakota County, and it was early in the morning of January 10, 1959. We had taken the Christmas tree down a few days before. My parents were in the barn with my father milking the cows and my mother washing the milking machines because she did a better job of cleaning than he did. The milk inspector came often to all the farms, and it was important to keep the Grade A standing when they sold the milk. My 5- year- old brother was asleep in my parents' bed, and my 10-year- old brother Mark was in his room getting ready for school. We rode the yellow school bus to St. Joseph's Catholic School in Rosemount. I was 13 and in the kitchen making breakfast.

"What time is it?" Mark yelled from his room.

"It is ten to eight," I yelled back, "Hurry up!"

And then I heard a noise which I was sure came from outside. I assumed it was the neighbor shooting at a rabbit or a skunk. I looked out the window to see if the O'Connors were nearby. And then my brother called my name, "Marilyn." His voice was scared--different, sort of.

I went to his room and opened the door, and he was lying on his back on the floor sort of moaning. I could see the wound in his stomach. I remember running outside through the snow to get my parents. I had no shoes on my feet.

My father told me to call an ambulance. Our telephone was on a party line with probably eight or so families. Two women were on the line, and whoever they were, they hung up immediately without even saying good bye.

The dispatcher at Sanford hospital in Farmington said an ambulance would be coming immediately. My parents knelt over my brother trying desperately to help but not knowing what they should do or if there was something that could be done. I remember letting the paramedics into the house and showing them where my brother was. My mother then went with the ambulance while I put clothes on my 5-year-old brother, and we then drove to the hospital with my father.

When we arrived, the hospital personnel almost inaudibly said that my brother hadn't made it. I either didn't want to hear that or couldn't believe what was being said. I asked the nurse to repeat it, and finally she clearly said he had died. Somehow that possibility had never occurred to me. Bleeding to death I would have understood, but there wasn't much blood. I don't think I comprehended at that time, that the damage was internal.

I had seen enough television to know that there was always the scene at the end of a show where the family gathered around the hospital bed, and the doctors said that it was touch and go for a while but the patient would be fine. All this happened in thirty minutes on television. Naive, maybe, but I hadn't experienced anything like this in my life. Remember too, that television was not as violent in the 50s as it is today. I wasn't able to think straight, I know. I remember going outside the hospital without a coat, and a person asked what was wrong and led me back inside the hospital.

We went home, and our relatives and friends came over--even relatives from Michigan and Indiana. People came, and I made lunches and coffee for so many. I know I liked being busy at that time because I desperately needed something to do. My mother was so shattered that I don't think she could have even made the coffee.

I remember one uncle trying to talk to me and treating me in such a juvenile manner. He meant well, but it was so apparent that he didn't know what to say and that he had never spoken to me other than to ask what grade I was now in . It just left me empty. And then another said how much better it was that my brother had died instead of being unable to walk and be in a wheelchair for his life. I didn't see it that way.

I remember my mother telling my aunt with nine kids that you can never have too many children. I remember my mother's sister telling my mother that if several people with troubles put all of their troubles in a basket, they would all take their own troubles back again. What a cruel thing that was to say. I remember bits of conversation, but a lot I just can't remember.

I remember listening to WDGY radio to give myself some relief. Listening to the radio was something that usually gave me some pleasure, but it didn't that day. I decided to remember the first song I heard, and make that song one that honored my brother. I think it was "green" something, but I am not sure I really heard it. It gave me no pleasure--nor any relief.

We had purchased that farm in April of the previous year. The house had been only three months old, and we'd had the barn built immediately. My parents felt they were doing pretty well. They had their family and a new farm.

We were not gun people. My father had owned a .22 rifle since before he married. It was used in case a skunk came after the chickens. In the rafters of the basement, however, the previous owners, the Adelmans, had left an 12 gauge shotgun. It was unloaded, but my father's brother had brought shells to try out the shotgun. The shells had been kept above my father's closet, up high so my 5- year old brother wouldn't get into them.

My father recalled a conversation while we had all watched *Gunsmoke* the previous Saturday night. Matt Dillon was loading his shotgun, and my brother asked how he put in the bullets. My father told him, and we continued watching the show without another thought. Earlier that Saturday, my brother Mark wanted pumpkin pie. It wasn't Thanksgiving, but my mother made it for him because he liked it and had asked for it.

The *Dakota County Tribune* came out on Thursday, their weekly publication date. There on the front page was the story of my brother's death. It read like fiction or yellow journalism. They had made up a quote from me that sounded as if I were a first grader.

Worse than that though, the reporter wrote, "Friends said he was retarded." I have worked toward a Ph.D. and my younger brother has a double major from University of California Berkeley. My brother Mark was no different than we were. He had B grades and a few A grades, and was in no way in any kind of special education classes. He read well and did math well too.   The article also said my father was abusive. My father was a gentle man and was in no way mean to anyone. No one had ever accused him of being anything except kind and always full of jokes.

How dare that reporter print stories that were so made up?   Didn't he realize that there was a family in such pain that his writing was just one more slap in the face? We could have sued, but I think we were just trying to survive after being so crushed. Had it been today or had I been older, I would have ever so royally gone after that reporter and his newspaper.

The article also said Mark had killed himself. Yes, but there are two meanings of that--intentionally or unintentionally. Did my brother commit suicide? I really don't think so. I think he was curious, and somehow the gun went off. Or perhaps he had watched television programs that showed everyone being well at the end. I have a master's degree in psychology and have had suicide prevention workshops over and over. I have worked with young potential suicides, and I conclude that my brother was not depressed. I have searched my mind over and over and can't think of any incident that would have told me he was having such thoughts. I will never know for sure, but there just were no signs.

I remember at the wake people repeatedly said that those who know you will know the truth, and the made up stories will make no difference to strangers. Not true. I think too that this incident made me study journalism and practice it with truth and care for every detail of every story I ever wrote or published.

The church was packed the day of the funeral. The children's choir sang, and I can remember nothing else from that day except walking down the church aisle after the casket as we were going to the cemetery across the street.

I remember going home, and no one came home with us. It was the first time that our family was alone. I remember I slept for awhile that afternoon. Being alone scared me.

I remember returning to school and walking into the classroom suddenly full of tears. The nun let me know that we would have none of that, so I stopped. No one ever talked to me about my brother. I guess I was supposed to pray. I think the students had been told to not mention the death to me because no one ever did. When I compare that with today, things are much healthier. On the news tonight there was a story about a fire in a science wing of a school, and the announcer said that a bevy of psychologists would be sent there to work with students.

No one ever said it aloud, but I felt that my mother had somehow wished that if she had to lose a child, it would have been me and not my brother. I think she thought that somehow I should have been able to prevent his death from happening. Never in a million years did I believe that my brother would have taken that gun out of the basement and found the shells that went into it. I thought he was putting his school clothes on. I started to blame myself at first but then realized that I could not control what I didn't know was happening. I was thirteen.

There were times in the months after that when I wasn't thinking straight. There were times when someone would comment that I was looking very intent and unknowingly shaking my head back and forth. There was another time when we had guests, and we were passing food around the table and suddenly I had put all the mashed potatoes from the serving dish on my plate instead of just one serving. I was mortified, but someone said to just put the extra back. I made a joke out of it, but I knew what was going through my mind. At this same time, I would find too much hair in my brush, My pretty hair was falling out and becoming a lot thinner.

It was never the same after my brother died. My parents seemed to get old awfully fast, and I remember many years later at the time of my father's death when he couldn't talk because he was full of tubes and he wrote, "I am going to be with Mark." I wonder in so many ways how life would be if none of this had ever happened and Mark had grown to be a man.

To this day, I am petrified of guns. There are none in our home--never even a squirt gun. I remember walking past stores with guns in the window and just being cold with fear I now avoid streets with gun stores. I have worked in inner city high schools, and I remember a phone call from a parent who asked me to check to see if her son had taken the gun from under her pillow because it was missing, but the gun from under her husband's pillow was still there.   I reacted smoothly and professionally, but all I could think was, "How stupid could you be? How can you sleep with a gun under your pillow?"

When I've heard students speaking ever so casually about guns, I have talked to classes about my loss. I speak to them generally and don't give them many details. They listen, and I hope to God, I have saved a life and saved another family such heartache.

Mark Mikulewicz
July 2, 1948-January 10, 1959

Grandma Beck
by Helen Tucker Chapman

I can still picture Grandma Beck wearing her gold-rimmed round glasses and her hair pulled back into a bun, sitting in her wicker rocking chair crocheting doilies and pot holders that I still have.

Helen Butenhoff came to the United States at age 7 in 1884 and married William Beck in 1902. Grandpa was born in Tinley Park, Illinois, and his birth records burned in the Chicago Fire. They raised three children in Waltham, and Grandpa died before I was born.

Grandma Beck lived alone in a little three-room house on Waltham's main street. She had a washroom off the kitchen that held a dry sink with a wash basin and a pitcher of water. A trap door led down to the cellar.

Also off the kitchen was an enclosed porch she called the shanty, where she kept her washtubs, broom, mop, pail, mattress for the outdoor swing, and a barrel where she kept fuel for the stove that sat in the middle of the kitchen and heated her house. Since Grandma didn't have a refrigerator, she used her shanty to store food and fresh milk during cold months, and also to make Jello. During warm months she used Carnation canned milk.

For years Grandma got water from the Schnirring Farm Implement store next door to her house. When she finally installed running water, it came from one kitchen faucet. She never had a sink with a sewer system, but I imagine the one faucet was a godsend after hauling so much water. Behind the house was an outhouse, and in the closet off her bedroom she kept a chamber pot that we used at night or during cold weather.

My earliest memory of staying with Grandma is of sleeping with her in her big four-poster feather bed. There was nothing more delightful than to crawl into bed and sink into that goose down, soft, fluffy feather mattress. Those feathers were later made into pillows, but the memory of how it felt to sleep on them will be with me forever. In the stillness of night, I could lie there and hear the "tick tock" and chimes on the hour and half hour from her large old clock that sat on a dresser in Grandma's kitchen.

I woke each morning to the smell of Postum coffee. What a memory! I can almost smell it now. Grandma let me have coffee along with a bowl of oatmeal and a piece of toast that she made over the flames of her kerosene burner stove.

She was a great German cook who always cooked my favorite foods when I stayed with her. Some of her specialties were sauerkraut and spare ribs, pork cutlets that were so tender you could cut them with a fork, beef roll ups with mashed potatoes and gravy, and graham cracker pie. All were prepared on a kerosene burner with a portable oven that she would put on top.

One of my favorite pastimes at Grandma's house was going into the barn on her property and looking through old trunks and boxes. Oh what treasures! Old clothes, hats, postcards, books and a never-ending supply of things to look at and examine kept me busy for hours. Sometimes she let me pull down a ladder from an opening in the ceiling of her closet and go up into her attic that contained more treasures.

The Great Western Railroad tracks ran right across the road from Grandma's house. My grandpa and both my uncles worked for the railroad, so it was always a big deal to run across the road and wave at the engineer, count the cars and wave at the conductor when the caboose went by. It was almost a ritual, and we did it for many years.

My Uncle Earl would sometimes come to Waltham to start his job with the railroad. Sometimes my cousin Roger would come along and stay at Grandma's during the day. Later in the afternoon, Grandma would let us walk around the railroad tracks to meet my uncle on the section car, and then he would let us ride the section car back to Waltham with him. I thought that was so exciting.

Grandma took me on the train with her when she went to Bolan, Iowa, to stay with Uncle Ray. One time during World War II we bought a whole suitcase full of marshmallows in Bolan because there weren't any to be had in Waltham.

Grandma always had time to play Chinese checkers with me. I remember choosing the color of marbles I wanted and setting up the game, but I don't remember if I won many games.

As clothing styles changed, Grandma never got used to short dresses and bare legs. Many times she spoke in part English and part German, rebuking my fashion sense, "Och himmel, I see your blanke arsch!" In English this meant, "Oh heavens, I see your bare ass!"

Grandma had a swing that stood in her backyard under a big tree. It was like a bed spring with chains on both ends that hung from a steel pole frame. Grandma put the stuffed swing mattress that she kept in the shanty on the swing, and on hot summer days she would give me a dime to run to the store and buy two bottles of cold pop. We would sit on the swing in the shade of the big tree and drink our cold pop and try to stay cool.

Grandma had many lady friends that we visited, or sometimes they visited her. Most were German, so they spoke German if they were talking about something they didn't want me to hear. One hot summer day Grandma and Lena Eggert were going to walk out to the Schmidt farm about a mile away to meet their son's bride that he had just brought home after the war. Grandma and Lena both had big black umbrellas to keep the hot sun off them. I thought it was stupid to walk under an umbrella on a nice day, and Grandma got upset with me. She kept saying I would have a sunstroke.

One time Grandma sent me on an errand, and when I came back, she wasn't around. For some reason, I hid behind the davenport. When she came back, she sat down in her rocking chair and kept saying to herself such things as, "Oh me, oh my. Where is that Helen?" I don't remember her reaction when I finally jumped out of my hiding place, but I don't think I ever pulled that trick on her again. I used to think it was so funny that she talked to herself. Now I talk to myself all the time, which I don't think is the least bit funny.

I wiped dishes that Grandma washed. In the morning when she made the bed, she would shake and shake the featherbed to fluff it up again.

She had an old push lawn mower, and I sometimes helped her mow the lawn. Every spring she took her rug from the living room and hung it up and beat the dust out. I don't remember how she washed her clothes, but I remember her ironing everything--sheets, pillowcases, towels, and even long cotton stockings and bloomers.

Going shopping with Grandma was a major event that required getting cleaned up and combing my hair. Grandma would change into her good dress, put on her hat that she usually wore whenever she went out, and get her purse and shopping bag. We walked to the store, which was about a block from Grandma's house. The store sold groceries, meat, some clothes and miscellaneous items. It was fun just walking up and down the aisles looking at everything.

Grandma had an old wind-up phonograph, and sometimes she let me turn the crank and we'd listen to records. On Sunday mornings I would have to be quiet so she could listen to a Sunday morning recorded church service with Reverend Fuller or Reverend Schuler--I'm not sure of the name.

She died in 1963, but these childhood memories of our simple but good times together will be with me always. Times have changed, but I only hope that I can leave my grandchildren with as many happy memories of their time with me as I have of those times with Grandma Beck.

Helen Chapman lives in Austin, where she enjoys embroidery, gardening and volunteering for the Red Cross and Austin Medical Center. She has two adult children and five grandchildren.

Grandma Beck

The Last Garden
by Helen Tucker Chapman

For as long as I can remember, my dad, Paul Tucker, planted an extensive vegetable and flower garden. In the '30s, '40s and '50s, his garden was a necessity because he had ten kids to raise. In the following years, however, as each of us grew up and left home, his family decreased, but his garden size did not. At the end of each growing season, especially as he grew older, he swore he wouldn't plant such a large garden next year--but he always did.

Dad's garden was his pride and joy. His whole life revolved around the garden season that began in early spring when he started seeds in little containers on window sills. Much to my mother's dismay, it was not uncommon to see a tomato plant on the bedroom dresser or beside the sink. When weather permitted, he would transfer his house plants to the hotbed he had built out of old boards and storm windows, and on Good Friday he'd plant potatoes. Garden season ended when everything was harvested and the soil was tilled and ready for next year

Everyone in our small town knew of Dad's flower and vegetable garden. If anyone wanted tomatoes, dill to make pickles or those first new potatoes, Dad could supply them. The animals also benefited from Dad's garden. He planted sunflowers so the birds could eat the seeds and built and supplied various bird feeders and a platform on a tree with corn for the squirrels.

Besides common vegetables, he planted okra, eggplant, rutabagas, parsnips, garlic, horseradish and Swiss chard. Mother found numerous ways to prepare these foods. She served beets, for example, as a fresh vegetable, beet pickles, beet jam and even beet cake.

The only thing Dad never planted was broccoli. When I questioned him, he said he didn't like it. President Bush, who once made a similar pronouncement, might have considered Dad one of his "thousand points of light."

At the end of each harvest our cellar was filled with bins of potatoes, squash, sacks of onions, crocks of carrots packed in sand, and row upon row of Mason jars filled with vegetables and fruits. We might not have had many clothes or material things, but we never went to bed hungry.

There was nothing more mouth watering than thinking about that first taste of Dad's sweet corn, or that first red, ripe tomato, or that first taste of strawberry shortcake. Sure, you could buy those things at the store, but they never tasted as savory or delicious as when they came from Dad's garden. Dad could have won blue ribbons at the fair, but he didn't want recognition.

On a calendar hanging in the hallway, Dad kept a daily record. Each day was marked with low and high temperature, cloud conditions, and the amount of precipitation. He noted seed plantings, when the first tomato was picked, and how many pints or quarts of strawberries or raspberries were picked. That calendar was like the Paul Tucker almanac.

One of Dad's greatest challenges was keeping raccoons from eating the tender ears of sweet corn. He spent hours erecting an electric fence to keep them out and building a box trap to catch them, but those efforts were to no avail. No matter what he did, the raccoons outwitted him. He trapped a raccoon once, but he let it out on the other side of town, and I'm sure it made it back for that night's feeding.

He was a quiet and independent man who never criticized his children or tried to run our lives. I can't remember him raising his voice to me, although there were times when it would have been appropriate--like the time I knocked one side of the garage off its foundation when I was learning to drive. He looked at me, then silently went about repairing the garage.

Although he was a friendly person, Dad's social life was limited. Every day he and his dog Tuffy drove to town where they'd stop at the post office, the grocery store and the local watering hole for a beer, some gossip and a little gambling. He seldom came to the homes of his adult children, but we were always welcome at his.

He was content with his routine, so it was obvious when Dad started feeling sick. He was losing weight and experiencing pain so in April he finally agreed to see a doctor. At age 81, he was admitted to the hospital for the fist time in his life. The diagnosis was cancer of the stomach and liver. Although the stomach cancer was operable, the liver cancer was untreatable. Dad elected to avoid surgery, go home, and just take one day at a time.

I took Dad home to get on with his life as normally as possible, and that, of course, meant getting the garden planted. Since he was very independent, he quickly and firmly refused offers of help. After all, he had planted a garden for 50 years on this same property, and this year was going to be no different.

He planted potatoes a few at a time, sitting on a pail to rest between planting the hills. He planted rows of seeds, sometimes on his hands and knees, and scattered flower seeds because he no longer had the strength or energy to make rows. It took longer than usual, but he didn't leave any ground unseeded. For Mother's Day, my sisters and I bought bedding plants and planted a flower garden near the house. We put flowers and trim along one side. Since it was a present to Mom, we were able to plant and take care of it without any objections from Dad.

In June my sister and I decided to go out and try to help Dad in the garden. He still found energy, from God only knows where, to push the rotor tiller with one hand while he steadied himself with the other. We told him that we would just pull the weeds around the plants that he couldn't get with the tiller.

When he got tired of pushing the tiller, he sat in his chair by the barn and watched us working in the garden. Every so often, he walked over to where we were pulling weeds and told us it was time to quit; just watching us made him tired. He said he would get it done when he felt better. Actually, I think he was checking on us to see if we really knew a weed from a plant and to make sure we weren't pulling any of his plants.

As I left that day and backed out of the driveway, Dad was sitting in his chair by the barn. There were tears in my eyes as he waved good-bye to me, for I knew this would be the last year there would be a big garden of vegetables and flowers that had been part of the homestead for years.

As the summer progressed, Dad made fewer objections when we came to help in his garden. One day, as we were pulling weeds, we tried to come up with a scheme to get Dad to let my sister use the rotor tiller. She went to the house and told Dad, "If she (meaning me) thinks I'm going to pull all those weeds one by one, she's crazy" A few minutes later, she came out of the house, followed by Dad, and he told her how to start and run the rotor tiller. To my surprise, she managed to go between the rows without digging up any of the vegetables or flowers.

Dad was getting weaker every day, but he totally refused to give up or admit gardening was getting too strenuous for him. He managed to dig some of the first crop of new red potatoes, a few hills at a time. He sat in his chair by the hotbed, where a few unplanted tomato plants still grew. As he sat in his chair, he saw the tomato plants blossom and grow into little green tomatoes. I wondered if he would be there to see them ripen. As I backed out of the driveway that day, he waved to me from his chair. There were tears in my eyes because I knew this would be the last year I would see Dad sitting in that chair by the barn.

We reaped the benefits of Dad's difficult labor of love. We picked string beans, cucumbers, raspberries, and pulled beets, onions and carrots. What a joy it was to see Dad pick his first ripe tomato from one of the plants in the hotbed by his chair! But by now Dad spent less time in his chair watching us working in the garden, which made me feel much less ill at ease. Seeing the pain, hurt, and tears in his eyes as he finally acknowledged the fact that he was unable to do any physical labor was almost unbearable.

Bouquets of roses, gladiolus, asters, daisies and assorted flowers were always arranged in vases on the kitchen table and on the TV. Fresh vegetables were served at every meal, and as my mom was not doing any canning this year, there were always plenty for us to take home when we were done working in the garden.

Now, when I backed out of the driveway, Dad was sitting in his chair by the window in the house as he waved good-bye. There were tears in my eyes as I realized it was not likely I would ever see Dad sitting in his chair by the barn again.

We harvested vegetables the same way Dad had done for years. We wiped the tomatoes with a cloth and put them in a cardboard box between layers of paper with stems removed and the top side down. The potatoes, carrots and cucumbers were washed and laid on the picnic table to dry. Onions were put in bags and hung in the barn to dry. Carrot tops and any discarded pieces were thrown on the compost pile.

Now when I left, Dad was either lying in his recliner or on the davenport. It took more energy now to raise his hand to wave good-bye. As I backed out of the driveway, Dad was no longer sitting in his chair by the window. There were tears in my eyes knowing that I would probably never see Dad's face in that window, sitting in his chair again. If Dad wasn't in his garden over all those years when I came home, seeing him in his chair by the window was as predictable as the sunrise in the east.

The calendar in the hallway was now void of Dad's handwriting. There were no recorded temperatures, no weather conditions, and no mention of any vegetables or pints of strawberries picked. The dates on the calendar looked as forlorn as a row of telephone poles out on a stretch of barren land.

There wasn't much left in the garden, but I picked the squash, which filled up the lawn cart. I pushed the cart to the back door, and somehow Dad found the strength to get to the door to see them. He smiled when he saw how many there were and told me to take a few dozen home. I checked the raspberries to see if they needed picking. Would they never quit producing? I picked some raspberries that day too.

As I prepared to leave, I went to Dad as he was lying on his bed. We held each other's hands, and we cried together. He thanked me over and over again for all the things I'd done, and we told each other good-bye. He knew and I knew that his days were numbered.

The first frost killed off any remaining raspberries and other vegetables. The vines and plants were pulled and thrown in a pile. After being instructed by Dad from his bed on the correct procedure, my sister dug up the gladiolus and other bulbs from the garden. I picked dried seeds from a variety of flowers that I saved to plant in my flower garden the next year as a memorial for Dad.

My dad, Paul Eugene Tucker, died on October 17. So ends the saga of his last garden. Amidst my tears, I knew someday I would smile because Dad left behind such wonderful memories. I knew I would smile whenever I saw a rose or ate fresh strawberries because those things would remind me of Dad. There will always be a place in my heart for Dad--and a special memory of that last summer with him surrounded by his last garden.

Paul Eugene Tucker

Christmas Eve Long Ago
by Caroline Feder

Dad had finished his evening farm chores early this special day for it was Christmas Eve, December 24, 1920. Even the milking was completed ahead of schedule, and we were excited. There was good reason for all this excitement; the Christmas Eve Sunday school program was scheduled to start at exactly six o'clock, which was usually our suppertime with chores following.

This evening we ate some of the bread that Mother had baked that day with homemade sausage, canned applesauce from the cellar and an assortment of freshly baked cookies, including pfefferneusse, a German delight. We lived on a farm about four miles from the village of Echo. The Borning family consisted of my parents and five children: Hazel, Willis, Caroline (myself) Bernard and Grace. Glenn and Lester completed the family sometime later.

Christmas Eve was clear and cold with a myriad of stars shining in celebration of the Savior's birth. The ground was covered with hard, crusty snow as the temperature had been zero and below. Dad readied the sleigh with about six inches of fragrant clean straw on the floor, and planks set on blocks made seats along the sides. Tony and Daisy, our team of horses, were brushed and curried to perfection in readiness for this journey to church.

Mother had sewed new Christmas dresses for us girls. Mine was bright red wool, befitting the season. Excitement reigned as we piled into the sleigh for we knew that Santa Claus would very likely visit our house while we were in church.

Because of the hard-packed snow, Dad decided to take a short cut and avoid the road. So over the fields we went, over fences deeply buried in snow. What fun! Then it happened. Dad turned a bit too sharply, and over we went. The sleigh turned on its side, and we were all thrown out in the snow with straw all over our pretty new dresses and us.

Dad righted the sleigh; Mother brushed off the straw and snow, and we were on our way again. We were not too boisterous at this point. When we reached the church and were in the lighted room, Mother finished her job of straightening our clothes and combing our hair, removing the last bits of straw. The program was about to begin so we hastened to our seats in the front of the church, hoping we would remember our recitations after our traumatic experience out in the snow. All went well, and the service ended with "Silent Night."

Then came the fun. Every child received a sack of goodies that included nuts, candy, an orange and an apple. Believe me, those were treats at that time.

Tony and Daisy were anxious to go and get back to their nice warm stalls in the barn so we started for home. This time there were no accidents, and we arrived home safely. The kerosene lamps were all lit, and there it was. Santa had not forgotten us. There was one toy for each of us, and the rest of the gifts were much-needed clothes. Mother, Santa's helper, had been busy with her treadle sewing machine for some time. We were almost too excited to sleep, but when Dad said, "Time for bed," we did not hesitate. Tomorrow would come and bring more fun.

This all happened so many years ago, and yet I still remember it clearly. What a wonderful night that was back on the farm near Echo.

Caroline Feder was a teacher, business woman and world traveler. She is now retired and living in Carlsbad, California. Her sister-in-law Anna Borning submitted this story.

Northfield's First Hockey Champs
by Steve Swanson

Too often today men's and boys' hockey relies on physical intimidation and sometimes flagrant unsportsmanlike conduct as a game strategy. Hockey was so tame back when I was a kid that none of us wore face cages–not even the goalie. Lloyd Harkness was our goaltender in the winter of 1947-48, the one and only year before the modern era when Northfield High School had a hockey team. Social science teacher Loyal Burmeister coached. It helped, of course, to start with a gentleman coach.

We set up a rink on the dam end of the Cannon River rink. Ozzie Simonich, shop teacher, welded up some goalie cages out of used pipe and covered them with chicken wire. We couldn't afford real boards so we borrowed bleacher planks and stacked them up around the perimeter of the rink. Any airborne puck more than eleven and a quarter inches off the ice would clear the boards and end up in the snow–or too often for Burma's slim budget, over the dam.

It's a miracle I got to play at all. I give my figure skating sister Marilyn and our long-suffering father half the credit. We skated on Hopkins ponds and Dad's home-flooded back yard rinks when I was little.

After three crucial years of no skating when we lived in Florida, I give the other half of the credit to Nancy Dvorak, my first infatuation. We skated together every winter night of my lonely eighth grade year on Powderhorn Park Lake. We played a lot of tag and pullaway--great for skating skills. Nancy broke my heart soon after and ended up marrying a St. Olaf graduate and Army career chaplain.

But I learned to skate, my broken heart healed, and as a sophomore I got to play on Burma's 1947-48 District Championship team. We earned that title by being that year the only high school hockey team in the district.

In the regional tournament, we lost to a strong Rochester team 10-1. We played on indoor ice–a first for almost all of us. It was like skating on foam rubber..

The score would have been 50-1 except for goalie Lloyd Harkness, who must have stopped 200 shots-- about ten of them with his face.

But hear this: We took second in the region. Rochester went on to the state tournament, and we came home with a regional second place trophy. Lloyd, one eye still swollen shut, got to present the trophy to Principal William Carlson in an all-school assembly the following Monday.

The second place trophy and our impressive regional achievement is part of Northfield High School's athletic history. Our second place victory would have been more impressive and satisfying, however, if there had been more than two teams in the region.

Steve Swanson is a retired St. Olaf English professor and an ordained Lutheran Minister.

Winter Thriving Skills
by Jacqueline Nasseff Hilgert

Everything I'm told I need to survive in snow-covered wilderness is either on my back or trailing behind in the plastic sled I've been pulling across frozen lake water ten miles shy of Canada. With each boot step, the crusted snow collapses under my weight with a muffled crunch. I figure I'm 500 crunches from camp when, out from the tree-lined shore, a cacophony emerges. Barking. The Huskies have spotted us warm-blooded adventurers who for the next week will share their shoreline in the Boundary Waters Canoe Area in northern Minnesota.

Varied in age, wilderness experience and physical ability, our group marches single file in low light toward a heated lodge tucked beneath towering pines at West Bearskin Lake. As my 13-year-old son Marc urges me forward, my enthusiasm for this near-arctic experience builds.

When we reach shore we are welcomed to camp by our winter dogsled adventure instructors, and we meet the lead musher, Stefan Straka, who cares for 36 Alaskan Huskies scattered around the dog yard. Our next stop is the lodge, 400 yards uphill, but its blazing wood stove isn't enough to entice us inside. For most of us, the dogs are the reason we've come.

We scatter to get close to the wolf-like animals. Although I've owned dogs my entire life, I walk cautiously. Huskies aren't wild, but they're not domesticated either; they are working dogs whose job is to run. An instructor who prefers we call him Shaggy shares important advice: "Don't let the dogs get loose. They're pack animals, and they will fight."

To my right a small dog is showing fangs to his blue-eyed neighbor. The iron chains that keep the dogs in place look like they were lifted from a tow truck. I pause for a breath then inch toward a black and white Husky named Little Bear. He jumps up and greets me with a kiss, his paws hitting me mid-chest while his tail stirs up a small cloud of snow. His greeting is in-your-face affection, the sum of a breeding equation that combines a healthy dose of strength with an equal amount of sweetness – a lot like the evening greetings I get from my teenage sons.

Curiosity satisfied, we head indoors. After dinner we gather around the fire to get acquainted and talk about why we've come. I listen to reasons.

"I've never experienced snow," says a young man from Phoenix.

"I've never been to Minnesota," replies a woman from Los Angeles.

"I wanted a personal challenge," says a woman with a girlfriend.

"I've always wanted to dogsled," is repeated by just about everybody else.

My decision to come arose from a New Year's resolution to yank myself out of my comfort zone as often as possible. I figured all I needed was an open mind, courage, long underwear and wool socks. No one seems too concerned about the cold except me – a native Minnesotan and self-proclaimed cold-weather wimp. "We'll talk about the cold tomorrow," an instructor promises.

Hearty Husky

The cooperative atmosphere nurtures conversation, laughter and friendship at the next morning's breakfast of blueberry pancakes and pork sausage. Before heading outside we get a lesson on frostbite and hypothermia. Beyond the glow of the wood stove, windows reveal gray sky and snow crystals looping around craggy pines, a prelude to a winter storm that promises fresh powder in which to run and play. Run and play? Since being frostbitten as a teen, I have defined "winter run" as a quick dash between heated building and warmed-up car.

I pull my attention back inside to hear how staying warm is incumbent on staying dry. How ironic that here, where the thermometer hovers near zero, sweating can lead to freezing to death. I layer up and rejoin the group on the frozen bay to learn the finer points of harnessing, hitching, steering, and most importantly, stopping a six-dog sled.

For centuries, dogs were the engines fueling Greenlandic transportation. As man moved west across the Arctic, dog teams hauled timber and lumberjacks in Canada and Alaska. Today sledding thrives mostly for sport, and dogs are revered for their agility and speed rather than their size and strength. Mushers favor Alaskan Huskies, the mixed-breed cousins of larger blue-eyed Siberian Huskies. Breeding has tightened the pads on their paws (good for trails), increased their speed and fostered an easy-going temperament. Dogs can be hitched to sleds single file (useful for narrow trails), in tandem (more powerful and easier to control), or in a fan hitch (popular on glaciers), where each dog is tethered to the sled independently.

Stefan walks us through dog handling techniques and explains the parts of the sled. We will take turns on sleds. I smile at Marc, knowing that underneath his ski mask he's smiling too.

Along the six-dog gang line, the dogs behind the lead are called point dogs, and the dogs closest to the sled are called wheel dogs. Alaskan Huskies weigh only 40 or 50 pounds, yet they run almost 10 miles per hour while pulling twice their bodyweight. The toboggan-style sled has a plastic bottom, runners on each side, and a canvas bag that forms a passenger shelter.

The driver stands at the back of the sled with one foot on each runner and a firm grip on the handlebar. Steering is simply a matter of shouting a few commands: "Gee" to veer right, "Haw" to turn left, "Whoa" to stop. A brake bar is positioned between the runners. To stop the sled, the driver steps on the brake while shouting, "Whoa!" with as much authority as chilled lungs will allow. While the dogs tug at their lines, the sled is held in place by a large, metal claw hook that's tamped into the snow. The combination of braking and shouting will bring the sled to a stop, but as long as dogs are attached, only a well-placed snow hook will keep it that way. Stefan "green lights" our first run.

Harnesses lie in the snow holding each dog's position on the gang line. As soon as Marc picks one up, the yard erupts in noise. I grab a harness and go in search of my dog and find him pacing in front of his kennel. It's nearly impossible to unhook the chain from the dog's collar, but when I toss off my mittens, the harness slips on easily but my fingers go from flexible to stiff in seconds. With the harness secure and a hand slipped under the collar, I pull my Husky off his front legs, and we run to the sled where the harnessed dog is connected to the gang line via neck and tug lines. Marc hitches his dog and runs for another; I fall to my knees in front of the lead dogs, exhausted.

While down, I'm definitely not out. During instruction, Stefan told us someone would need to stay at the lead during harnessing to keep the dogs calm. Already on all fours, I figure I'm in the right spot to model good behavior to Monkey and Jillian. I pat both Huskies on the head while Marc hitches the rest of the team.

The barking continues as we prepare to start the run across West Bearskin Lake and through a wooded portage leading onto Pine Lake. There we'll stop the dogs so driver and passenger can switch positions. We'll continue the length of the lake, cross a road and drive the team back across West Bearskin toward camp. The run should take half an hour.

Marc and I head to our assigned sleds and jump into the passenger bags. Stefan takes the lead sled onto the lake. The rest of us wait for the signaler to pat his head, our cue to run. As soon as my driver Stephanie gets her cue, she pulls up the snow hook and we're moving.

A strange calm overtakes the dogs as we tear across the lake, and the only noise is the whisper of snow trailing off paws. I feel like I've been transported back to the time of Marquette and Joliet. Stephanie calls the dogs by name, encouraging them as they pull us across the wide expanse of frozen water. When we reach the portage between lakes, I get a sense of our speed as we tear past snow-laden pines. Before I know it, we're coming to a stop. I must turn my attention from scenery to steering. The dogs watch us change spots, giving a lurch or two to make it interesting.

With Stephanie settled, I yank up the iron snow hook and we're off again. My focus is on the dogs and the distance between them and the team just ahead. I can't let my team close in or I could get into trouble; the dogs could ignore my stop command, and if they catch the team in front, chances are a fight would ensue. We reach the road during our second portage, where surprised cross-country skiers watch us. Had they expected dogsleds flying over the road then disappearing into the trees when they'd set out for a snowy afternoon's glide?

Re-kenneling the dogs after our run is a low-key affair. Stefan doles out a meal of beef and fat mixed with water for the Huskies while we head uphill to find platters heaping with potatoes on our dining table. After we've eaten, we stay close to the fire to talk about the run. With adrenaline-spiked enthusiasm, we come to a quick consensus: Dog sledding is absolutely the coolest thing we've ever done!

A Metaphor For Life

Another day of heavy snowfall starts with French toast, eggs and bacon. Our meals are high in calories and fat because our bodies expend more calories in cold weather. The group splits for a day outdoors, and I join Shaggy as he leads a snowshoe trek across the lake to Caribou Rock with a breathtaking view of West Bearskin Lake.

As we ascend the trail, Shaggy says, "I think of dog sledding as a metaphor for life." The crystallized moisture from his breath clings to his yellow beard.

"A metaphor for life? What do you mean by that?" I press, wondering what this 24-year-old man has seen that produces insights associated with middle age.

"You can get lulled into thinking you've got everything under control, and you never do," he answers. "You're out on a trail, 10 maybe 20 miles from home, and everything's going great. All of a sudden a porcupine crosses your trail. By the time you get the sled stopped and tied down, the dogs have devoured the porcupine and half your team has quills stuck in their faces. You have to pull the dogs off the gang line, wrap them in a blanket to keep them still and tie them into the sled. Guess who's pulling the sled now?" I ponder that image the rest of the way uphill.

We slump into the snow when we reach Caribou Rock and take turns with cameras and a communal sack of raisins and peanut mix known as gorp. The wind buffets the ridge, and body heat quickly dissipates. We head down the trail toward camp, dinner, and a full-stoked wood stove.

Canine Freight Train

The path from the lodge to the bay bends slightly left then straight downhill. It's about 6:45 a.m., and the snow is slicing across the dog yard at a 45-degree angle. I pause at lake's edge and look west across the ice. The horizon line of trees that separate the inevitabilities of a Minnesota winter – frozen lake from dismal sky – has been erased. A massive low-pressure system has rendered 100 acres of 200-year-old pines invisible.

The Huskies hear human activity and shatter the silence. Stefan, who has prepared four sleds for the early run, asks if I can take the driver's spot on sled four. Shaggy senses my hesitation and volunteers. I spot Marc crouched near Little Bear. Marc is not scheduled for the run, but prefers the dog yard to bed this morning.

Three sleds wait in a line on the path that intersects the yard between the lake and bay. On the bay end of the path, drivers must ace a 90-degree turn off an icy embankment to reach the center of the bay where the path diverges. The signaler stands at this hinge and gets a great view as the sled driver bends low and leans heavily into the turn. If the driver doesn't lean heavily enough, the sled rolls over, and the signaler is well positioned to aid the team.

There isn't room for four sleds on the path, so the lead sled rests out on the bay facing the spot where the trail splits off into the woods. Instinctively, the dogs won't run right at a person; if they see someone blocking the back trail, they will run across the lake – Stefan's chosen course. Three days ago, Stefan had his pick of signalers and trail blockers to help the sleds get out of the yard without incident. This morning he has only Marc and me; most campers are lingering inside well past breakfast following an optional sans tent sleep-out in the snow. Marc sprints to the far end of the bay and becomes guidepost for 24 Huskies. I stay in the yard to signal drivers. A glance at the thermometer tells me it's warmed up to 15.

I wait for each driver to pat his head. Then I signal Stefan, and before I know it, he's around the shoreline, barely visible. I pat my head, and the second driver bends over to yank out his snow hook. The dogs stop barking and jerk the sled onto the bay. When the second sled disappears on the lake, I signal the third.

It's quieter in the yard with only six dogs, and I'm grateful their turn is coming. The wind has been cutting right through my fleece pants. I pat the top of my head and see Shaggy bend over to pull up his snow hook. Six dogs tear up the path right at me. I notice they're running faster than the other three teams. Then I notice Shaggy just over the wheel dog's hindquarters–he hasn't moved. The gate latch at the end of the gang line had sprung open, and the team is loose.

Shaggy yells up the path, "Stop them, stop them!" Then begins the chase. I step into their path, hoping they'll stop for me, but they zoom right by. I try to grab the rope dragging behind the wheel dogs, but it's past me before I can blink. I'm amazed by their speed. I yell to Marc, "Stop them! Stop them!"

Because of new-fallen snow, it seems like I'm running in slow motion. Beyond Marc lies the white expanse of West Bearskin Lake, and beyond that, hundreds of square miles of wilderness. Marc runs straight at the team, screaming "Whoa! Whoa!" with a voice so deep I hardly recognize it. The dogs ignore his commands, invigorated by the weightless sled they're pulling. When Marc intercepts the team, he throws his body across the middle dogs. This defensive football tackle slows them enough that I reach the trailing rope.

My mitten-covered hands aren't giving me any leverage against the dogs so I wrap the rope around my arm, dig in my boots and try to become a human snow hook. Huskies can pull twice their bodyweight, and the irony isn't lost on me in the middle of this frozen bay as Marc and I are losing a tug-of-war to six 45-pound dogs. Seconds later a breathless Shaggy appears at the head of the team, and I find confidence that we can save the dogs from their own instinct. Marc is yelling, "Whoa! Whoa," and I gain enough slack to make another rope loop around my arm.

Shaggy shouts his plan. "See that tree? "We're going to move them over there and tie them up." The dogs are still inching us toward the lake when we agree that we're going to try moving this canine freight train sideways toward the tree. We pull and pull, and the dogs start scrapping with each other. Shaggy and I keep pulling. Marc, who's caught up in the tangled gang line, keeps our frustrated dogs from tearing each other apart.

About every third or fourth step I sink into the thigh-deep snow and end up on my knees. This slows us down, but we progress toward shore. When we reach the tree, Shaggy shouts, "Wrap the rope around the trunk two times, then tie it up!" I have to toss off my mittens to grip the rope. I get it around the trunk once before I realize my heart is pounding its way out of my chest. It's not enough. "Put it around again!" Shaggy shouts. The rope is caked in snow, but somehow I manage to get another loop around the tree trunk. "Can you tie it off?" he asks.

"Yeah." It's a response born of sheer will. My fingers barely function, and my attempt fails. Seeing me struggle, Shaggy asks if I can hold the rope until he can come around and tie it off. While Shaggy makes his way around the tree, my focus stays on the rope. It doesn't stop slipping until the knot is in place. The dogs accept defeat. We look at each other, too breathless for words, as six Huskies, tied to each other and to a tree, look at us not understanding what just happened; they were doing their job.

When his panting slows, Shaggy asks, "See what I mean – about this being a metaphor?" I nod, then look past him toward the lake and beyond, toward home, thinking about instinct and how it spurs movement. A wind gust causes suddenly sparkling sheets of snow to rise from the sur-face and glide across the ice like trans-parent sailboats, a surreal symmetry of grace and motion I can embrace only now that I've forgotten I'm cold.

Marc and Shaggy unhook each harness to walk dogs back to their kennels. Until they're done, I sit comfortably under the tree and talk to the Huskies. "It's OK," I tell them, patting their heads. "You'll get to run later…I know you're good dogs. That's right! You're gooood dogs."

Jackie Hilgert, a writer who appreciates adventure, travel, photography, and thick wool socks, lives in Bloomington with her husband, twin sons, and a large furry dog.

All There
by Marian Westrum

It was a Saturday morning in early February, 1941, and I was alone in my office in the Albert Lea Junior College building on Lakeview Boulevard. The janitor had finished his chores and gone home almost as I had arrived. The dean, my boss, had not come in. Occasionally, one of the teachers would come in to finish up some odds and ends of work, but this morning nobody came in—the phone had not even rung.

I had transcribed a letter that I had taken just before 5 o'clock last evening and completed the final few entries in the cash journal that lay open before me on the desk. I could not think of another task needing to be done. My eyes strayed to the engagement ring on my finger, and I thought about Lyle. I met Lyle Westrum as a teenager in our neighborhood on Abbot Street, and we were high school sweethearts. We were engaged to be married on June 14, 1941.

Lyle was first, last, and always an athlete. He spent all his spare time at the hockey rink. It was lucky for me, I mused, that the general skating rink was near the hockey rink so that occasionally he'd come over and skate with me during his evening hockey practice.

I thought about tomorrow. Albert Lea would take to the ice against Rochester, last year's Southern Minnesota League champs, in the final game of the season. These were city hockey teams, and towns like Mankato, Faribault and Austin made up the league. The teams were all tied up in the standings this season so the final game was critical. Little shivers of excitement went through me because Lyle was the star of the team. He could skate rings around anyone I had ever seen on skates. With the puck on the ice and the hockey stick in his hands, nobody but nobody could make more goals than he. And it wasn't a one-man show either— he knew how to pass and maneuver around that rink and make the whole team work together.

An insistent noise jarred my thoughts. Oh, the phone! It was for me. Mr. Larson, the personnel man at Wilson's meat packing plant where Lyle

worked, was on the line. What was he saying? At first I couldn't comprehend. Lyle had been hurt, had been taken to the hospital and was asking
for me. I was to come at once . . . hurt where? . . . his right hand had been
torn horribly in a stripping machine . . . possible surgery . . . maybe re-
moval of the hand . . . Oh, no. At the very least, hundreds of stitches. Yes,
yes, I could come to the hospital immediately.

The phone banged on the desk. I replaced it on its cradle absently, my
mind racing elsewhere. There was only one thing I must do now, but I
could not make myself respond, I thought. I looked-- my desk was all in
order—I even had on my coat and overshoes and was tying my kerchief. I
slung my purse over my arm and held the key in my hand to lock the door
as I went out. I looked at the clock, but it was the wrong time for the bus.
I would have to walk several blocks.

That it was a beautiful February morning was not entirely lost on me for
I had enjoyed my walk to work through the new fallen snow. We had had
a thaw earlier in the week, though, and here and there under the snow
were patches of ice where the melting snow had refrozen. The air was
crisp, and I breathed deeply to clear my whirling brain.

My thoughts kept pace with my brisk walk. How, how had it happened?
What had Mr. Larson said? Stripping machine roller covered with
burlap...strings hanging from burlap...Lyle had reached to remove a string
hanging, but this wasn't to be done without first turning off the machine.
What had happened? Perhaps he too had been looking ahead to tomorrow.
Anyway, it had happened, and in a moment this incident could change his
whole life.

After I slipped and almost fell I slowed my pace. I couldn't run all the
way. By now I was approaching Dane Lake. Should I risk crossing it?
The ice underneath would be honeycombed from the thaw and then the
freeze. I would risk it because it cut off so many blocks and would take
me to the back door of our house on Pleasant Avenue. I must stop and tell
Mother. Anyhow, it was very close to noon, and she would be expecting
me. I hurried along the path, slipping and sliding. A couple of times a
foot went through the ice, but I made it and dashed up the back steps.

"Mother," I called urgently, "Lyle has been hurt—his right hand. I'm going to the hospital." She came at once and threw her arms around me. "Oh, Mother, what will he do—his right hand." At last the tears came. She soothed me as if I were a small child again. I would call her later. Perhaps, just perhaps, the whole episode had been exaggerated. I prayed that this was so, but in the back of my mind a little voice whispered, "Mr. Larson would not have misled you."

I walked, I ran, stumbled, and almost fell a couple of times. Thank goodness the path along the railroad tracks was clearly visible under the light film of new fallen snow. I reached Fountain Street at last, three more blocks to the hospital door. The girl at the desk said Lyle was just out of surgery. Surgery. My heart skipped a beat, but of course they would call it surgery even if they had not cut off his hand.

The hall was endless. Dr. Donovan, the plant doctor, stopped me. "We were able to sew up the hand. He wouldn't take the anesthetic until Dr. Neel and I promised him we would not amputate."

I was then at his bedside, my arms around Lyle. He was crying and talking all at once. And he was holding up his bandaged hand and counting over and over, "1, 2, 3, 4, 5. 1, 2, 3, 4, 5." Finally he said, "They are all there. They are all there." Lyle was lucky. Although his many stitches created a permanent scar, his injury didn't cause any long term physical pain or movement restriction. He didn't have to sit on the sidelines.

This brush with tragedy brought the two of us even closer, and we got married on our scheduled day in June. Lyle resumed playing hockey the next winter, but his sports activities were interrupted again--this time by Uncle Sam. After a stint in the Army, Lyle returned to me. We had two children and lived 49 years as husband and wife until his death in 1990.

Albert Lea resident Marian Westrum has two adult children, two grandchildren, and two step grandchildren. She used to play a fine game of golf.

Lyle Westrum

A Minnesota Exotic
by Julie Westrum King

I was in second grade at McKinley School in Faribault when Hawaii became a state. My teacher, Miss Walacha, who had recently vacationed there, introduced us to many things Hawaiian. In so doing, she taught us the word "exotic." Hawaii was exotic, she said; it was beautiful, colorful, out of the ordinary, striking, unusual. Though I hadn't heard the word before that day in school, and I hadn't been anywhere farther away than Iowa, I knew all about exotic--my aunt Maxine was exotic.

"Where are we going, Max?" my five-year-old self asks. The car windows are down, the day is hot, and I am glad for the breeze. We stop at a red light; Max adjusts the knot of her scarf, looking in the rear view mirror. I don't know how she keeps it on the tip of her chin like that. As the light changes to green, she slips her foot out of her sandals, and I watch her bright red toenails as she presses on the accelerator. Max like to drive barefoot!

"Well, we have some shopping to do, and then maybe ice cream?" Her blouse is as red as her toenails. She has stitched together two bandanas to make a sleeveless top.

"I like your shirt, Max."

She smiles and gives my ponytail a little yank. "Thanks. It took me about five minutes to make."

One of my father's younger sisters, with no children of her own, my aunt Maxine lavishes attention on me, and I adore being with her. Her house in Albert Lea is full of ultra modern blond furniture and beautiful things like ashtrays in abstract shapes and little stylized Chinese figurines. Her house is bright and airy, a modern ranch style. And she is always making something beautiful. Her sewing room is full of colorful fabrics and trims. I love looking at the patterns, imagining Max in the styles shown. She sews her own clothes, as well as gifts for people and things for the house like drapes and bedspreads.

She is especially adept at needlework, but creative in other ways, too. Right now she is in a candle-making phase. She does swirly, glittery things with tapers that end up so beautiful I am afraid of touching them.

On another summer day in the late 50s, Max picks me up in the morning and tells me to put my ice skates in the car. We are going up to Minneapolis to go skating indoors! But before we do that, we are going shopping-- indoors, too. There is a new place called Southdale, Max tells me, where there are lots of stores all under one roof. "It's called a shopping center," says Max. "It's amazing. They have birds in cages two floors high, and lots of escalators."

That makes me a little nervous. There is an escalator in Skinners' department store downtown in Albert Lea, and I am always a little hesitant about getting on and off. I get over that soon, because we go up and down all over Southdale. I don't remember if we bought anything, but I remember the birds and all the plants (even trees!) growing indoors and the new sleek water tower outside. Pointing at it, Maxine says, "There's Paul Bunyan's golf ball all teed up."

That gets us laughing. We have great fun skating too. It's cold in the big building, but we don't need winter coats; a sweater and long pants keep us warm enough. Max can do fancy skating. I love to watch her. I practice skating backwards, which means I fall and get up over and over, which gets us laughing again. We laugh and laugh all day. At least, that's the way I remember it.

My exotic aunt Maxine seemingly could do anything. She is a marvelous and adventurous cook who introduced me to exotic foods like Brussels sprouts, broccoli, avocado, sweet and sour (which I love), and curry (which I don't). I've eaten authentic sukiyaki at her table.

Her needlework created a sweater each year for me for many years, always in a beautiful unusual color or style. When I was in college, she sent me a crocheted poncho that was the envy of my hippie friends. She loves to travel and married a Navy man, so she has lived everywhere from Japan to Virginia.

And just when I thought she had settled into quiet middle age, she CLEPped two years of college, earned a master's degree and started her own counseling business. She is amazing.

Today is the first warm day in May. I can tell that vacation will soon be here—as welcomed by us teachers as it is by the students. I dig my sandals out of the back of the closet and choose a light dress to wear to school. Before breakfast I grab a bottle of nail polish and officially say hello to summer in my own way. I do it with a smile at the memory of a laughing young woman driving barefoot into an adventurous afternoon. It always makes me feel a bit daring. You see, every summer when I paint my toenails—though mine are apt to be hot pink instead of red—it is my little ritual in homage to my exotic Minnesota aunt.

Julie Westrum King was born in Albert Lea and lived in Faribault, New Ulm, Sioux Falls and Sheldon. She has one adult daughter and teaches high school English and drama in Wauwatosa, Wisconsin.

The Busboy House
by Edgar Simmons

Returning from my 50 year high school reunion, at an altitude of 35,000 feet on a United flight bound for my home in California, I put aside my book and found myself reflecting on the events of the past half century.

Three weeks after graduating from A.H. Parker High School, the largest of two high schools for Negroes in Birmingham, Alabama, my twin brother Allen and I headed for Minneapolis in the Negro section of the train. We chose to study at the University of Minnesota because we applied and they accepted. We didn't know anybody there, but we wanted to be independent, and our parents went along with the idea.

After three days on the train, we arrived in Minneapolis. Not knowing where the University was in relation to the train station, we checked with the person at the information desk. Since we didn't have much money, we decided to walk a few miles east to the University of Minnesota.

Reaching the campus, we wandered around the area looking for student housing. Within the hour, we came upon this big, brown three-story house with a sign in the living room window that said, "Rooms for Rent." When I rang the doorbell twice, a tall young man named Sanford Mickelson opened the door.

"Do you have a room large enough for two?"

"Yes," he said, "we do," and he took us to the second floor to a north-facing room with bunk beds. After looking at the bathroom down the hall, we put down a deposit on the room.

We spent about an hour in conversation with Sanford, learning about his background, telling him about our situation, and asking many questions about the university. One of the main things we wanted to know was how to go about getting jobs. Sanford, a graduate student, told us that most of the guys renting from him and his mother worked at University Hospitals for meals. The job involved replacing regular kitchen help on weekends, and serving three meals a day Saturdays and Sundays.

For this weekend work, busboys got three meals seven days a week, which they would eat in the hospital cafeteria along with the doctors, nurses and interns. Allen and I thought this sounded too good to be true. Later that evening Sanford introduced us to some of the other guys who rented from them and worked as busboys, and they promised to talk to the head dietitian about us getting on as busboys.

The next thing we had to do was look for regular paying jobs to do during the week. Off we went to the student employment office, where someone helped us. My brother was hired as a hospital orderly, and I became a clerk at Nicholson Hall Bookstore.

Six of the eight of us in the house worked as busboys, so everyone called it the "busboy house." We befriended some of our classmates and other busboys from the neighborhood. Most Friday nights, after a week of classes and work but before our weekend jobs at the hospital, we would gather at our favorite watering hole in Dinkytown to chug-a-lug a few beers.

I joined the football marching band, playing alto saxophone. I witnessed discrimination in the band because only guys could be members. Marching band required a huge time commitment to practice music along with learning choreography for rigorous halftime shows. Not only did we have to sound good, we had to be able to march with exaggerated steps and be in a special spot at a certain point in the music. Women were thought to be too frail to do all this, so they were not allowed to be part of this group.

Performing was fun until we had to provide halftime entertainment in the snow. This happened more than once. We tried to play our instruments with snow falling on our hands that were covered with white cotton gloves. The heat from our hands would melt the snow and freeze our hands. I could not press a key on my saxophone at one game. Sometimes when the weatherman predicted bad weekend weather, we would tape our music on Thursday, and they would play it over the public address system at halftime on Saturday. One time the weatherman was wrong, and Saturday afternoon weather was lovely. We had not planned to perform, so they played the taped music despite the nice weather, and this didn't go over too well with fans who enjoyed watching our halftime performances.

After two years we started to run short of funds to pay our expenses. Out of state tuition kept going up so my brother and I put our heads together and came up with the idea to apply for Minnesota residency. Paying resident tuition helped us out for awhile, but we were still scrambling to keep up. We decided to go to the Selective Service office and have our names put on the next call-up list for the Army. We figured this was better than volunteering for the Army because draftees only had to serve two years, whereas volunteers had to serve four years.

When we returned to Minneapolis two years later, we found that things had changed dramatically, and the jobs we left when we went into the Army were no longer available. We decided to move to Mankato, 90 miles away, and attend Mankato State. I enjoyed my studies and social life in Mankato, but the only job I could find was that of a weekend janitor at a Minneapolis hospital. So for two years I drove from Mankato to Minneapolis to do janitorial work. I stayed with any friend who would put me up for a couple of nights.

On August 22, 1961, I received my Bachelor of Arts degree from Mankato State College. I had accomplished my objective, but without my excellent start as a college man living in that big brown three-story busboy house, I don't know if I would have been able to make my way.

Ed and Allen Simmons, 1953

In 1995 I went back to Minneapolis as a representative for the National Education Association, and much to my disappointment, I saw that the busboy house had been torn down to make way for a parking lot. I suppose this would be regarded as progress by some people, but I would have been happy to have seen that old busboy house one more time.

Ed Simmons taught art and theater in Los Angeles County for 30 years. He is now retired and living in Vallejo, California.

Boundary Waters Adventure
by Gene Grazzini Jr.

Christmas, 2000, Greg puts a note in my present, an invitation to renew old memories of good times in the Boundary Waters Canoe Area. He says he'll guide. There was no way I was going to give up an opportunity to spend a few days with my son in one of the most beautiful parts of the world.

He asks, "Who'd you like to bring along?"

I suggest Steve, Donny and my grandson Shane.

Greg agrees. We wonder if Shane will enjoy it and be able to keep up, but we anticipate a great time. I'll have my two sons-in-law, my son and grandson with me; it doesn't get much better than this.

I put together my usual extremely well-documented trip list that always gets ridiculed by my daughters. They laugh, but for some strange reason crucial things are not left behind.

Wednesday evening, June 6, the group assembles. We build a canoe rack on top of my car carriers. Donny ties down the canoes with the skill of a master seaman. We may look like a capsized pontoon boat going down the highway, but our rack sure beats dragging a trailer.

Greg demands repacking to accommodate our food. Everyone protests that their pack is full, but Greg keeps right on stuffing packs and finally fits in everything. The back end of the Suburban is loaded, and everyone has his own personal stash of goodies. Donny brings freeze-dried tuna and unsalted sunflower seeds. Shane has gummy worms. Denise, one of my finest daughters, sends sugar cookies and snickerdoodles.

With the Burb loaded by 9:15, we spend quality time at the kitchen table relating tales of past Boundary Waters trips. Shane gets an anticipatory gleam in his eyes, Donny stresses about his food supply, Greg runs to Byerly's for sandwich fixin's, and Steve and I hang loose.

At 10 I read the packing list amidst guffaws and cat-calls. I'm sure glad my daughters were able to attend the recitation. By 10:15 we're off, and I take the first driving shift. At Hinckley I pull off the freeway and turn the wheel over to Greg. Next thing I know we're in Two Harbors at an all-night Holiday station, and its 2 a.m.

The Holiday clerk says there's nothing open north on 61 until 6. By 3, I'm back at the wheel as we pull into the ranger station in Tofte. It isn't scheduled to open until 6, so with little urging we all settle in for a nap. Who had the idea to depart at 10 p.m.?

We share the parking lot with other canoe-laden vehicles with sleeping occupants. I wake up at 5:30. We use the outhouses waiting for the station to open. I tell Shane this is his last chance to use an indoor toilet, but I don't think he quite understands yet.

At 6 on the dot, a lady ranger comes out to raise the American flag. We stare bleary-eyed as she hoists it to full mast, then like puppy dogs we follow her back into the station, making sure no one gets in line ahead of our crew.

The ranger gives the customary Boundary Waters sermon, complete with video. Raptly we listen because she's threatened us with a test. With a little sidelines kibitzing, Shane passes the test for our group. Greg receives our plastic waste bag, we pay the toll, and we're off. Wait! Donny asks after noticing a water spigot on the building. "Is that water sanitary to drink?" The ranger says it is.

Donny makes a dash for the car to get two five-gallon plastic containers and proceeds to fill them. As they fill, the water takes on a yellowish cast, and Donny gets uneasy. "Do you think it's okay?"

We assure him that it's just a trace of iron ore. Donny appears apprehensive, but keeps filling those containers. Steve, Greg and I glance at each other with the same thought. He really isn't going to haul those containers over the portages when there's good drinking water in the lakes we'll be traveling through.

Greg says, "You want it, you carry it."

Donny says, "Don't worry, I'll carry 'em."

Nothing opens in Tofte until 7, so finally we begin the winding trek up the Sawbill Trail to Brule Lake, the Boundary Waters. Everyone pitches in, anxious to get on the water and follow Greg to who knows where. By 8 we're paddling across Brule Lake looking for a portage six and a half water miles west.

We're fresh, the water is flat, and we're enjoying the invigorating feeling of muscles loosening up as we rhythmically dip our paddles in pristine waters. Steve and I with Shane in the middle, with a larger and heavier canoe, are leaving Greg and Donny in our wake. Donny hasn't quite accomplished the paddle stroke, and their smaller canoe appears to be slightly bow heavy.

We see the first signs of devastation from the straight line wind and storm of 1999. On the hilltops, the trees are toppled in twisted disarray. In places it appears that the storm never touched a leaf, while in other areas everything has been beaten down. The folks who were there when the brutal and terrifying storm came through must have been scared out of their wits with absolutely no shelter. They couldn't get into the lake, and they couldn't hide in the woods. It's amazing that no one was killed as huge uprooted trees slammed down with a vengeance.

We take on our first 100-rod portage (16 feet per rod) to Cam Lake with enthusiasm. Greg and Steve haul canoes while the rest of us hoist backpacks. The uneven footing causes Shane to stumble and trip three times, but he keeps going. Two trips get all our gear across, with Donny hauling two plastic containers of yellow water. Shane is a real trooper carrying his backpack across then doubling back to get another load.

We're back into canoes for a half-mile paddle north on Cam Lake. Portage #2, 45 rods to Gasket Lake, should be a piece of cake. We make it across with not quite the enthusiasm as our first portage, but we're not complaining. Donny totes his yellow water across, then goes back to get his backpack.

One mile north on Gasket Lake, we approach portage #3, 75 rods to Vesper Lake, with far less fervor; this is beginning to approach real work. Someone mumbles, "Only three more portages to go." Greg doesn't say anything. We step around rocks, balance on downed timber, slosh through mud, swat mosquitos, and haul our gear from one lake to another.

It's a short quarter mile west to portage #4, which looks impassable with downed timber. I send Greg ahead to look for chainsaw work. After a short hike he yells back that trees have been cut. It's 110 rods of downed trees, immense boulders, and muddy ruts. Just what we needed, a real challenge! After our two trips across, we put in to Town Lake paddling west for our next portage.

The 10-rod portage into Cherokee Lake is challenging. Paddling west on Cherokee is a respite, leaving the rocks, mud, trees, and mosquitos behind for a short time. Steve, Shane and I paddle north a quarter mile looking for a water passage to Gordon Lake. The map hinted that we might find one. No such luck! We turn around and paddle a quarter mile back, with Steve grumbling.

The 15-rod portage into Gordon Lake is the easiest so far. We cross without incident and put in for our three-mile paddle to our next portage. The weather has been beautiful with sunshine, very little wind, and some light overcast.

Portage #7 is only 28 rods long, an anticipated pleasure until we find that it is one of the most difficult. We struggle across knowing that we've only got one left, and it's only five rods.

Finally, we reach Long Island River that empties into Long Island Lake, where Greg says we can set up our tents. After a short paddle, we cautiously approach the short portage around the rapids that tumble into Long Island Lake. If we can remove some fallen trees, we should be able to run the rapids. We maneuver our canoes so Steve can pass his short handsaw over to Donny. Donny gets up on the timber jam and like a true lumberjack starts sawing and throwing logs off the jam.

With a final surge of muscle, Donny lifts an immense log off the jam that enables us to squeeze our canoes through the opening and enjoy an invigorating ride down the rapids.

We made it to Long Island Lake! Now we've got to locate a campsite. There are 16 on the lake, but they all seem to be occupied. We paddle east a couple miles and finally find a campsite. We've had enough paddling and portaging for one day. We want to get our tents set up, get dinner started and just relax.   Everyone pitches in getting firewood and setting up tents.

We relax around the campfire as Greg prepares our dinner of spaghetti and hamburger. After a long, challenging day, we're pleasantly tired, maybe a little over tired.

Donny is happy with all the pasta but opens freeze dried tuna fish and proceeds to devour the whole package. We wash dishes and pack it in for the night. Donny and Greg are in one tent, and Steve, Shane and I are in the other.

I'm up at 7:15, and a short time later Greg crawls out. I've already got a fire going, and my coffee water is boiling. I'm happy, the weather is beautiful, the water is flat, and we're in the BWCA. The serenity and beauty of early morning on a wilderness lake with the sun attempting to penetrate the light morning fog is my idea of heaven on earth. Greg fixes us a breakfast of freeze-dried Denver omelet. It is adequate and not heavy to portage in. After breakfast Steve makes a run to the head and almost gets carried away by mosquitos

At 9:30 we're in our canoes fishing. Donny picks up two small northerns, and the rest of us strike out. We break for lunch as Greg heats up soup. While the others nap, Donny and I go out fishing. As is my habit, I keep a weather eye on the sky, noting a few black clouds beginning to darken the west. I tell Donny, "We better head back before the storm catches us out on the lake," and we turn and paddle south, eyeing the sky, and once in a while tossing a cast or two.

All of a sudden, off our left shoulders, a bald eagle swoops within ten feet, then floats up to a tall pine in front of us. Donny whips out his trusty camera and starts taking pictures at very close range. We paddle on with a bit more determination as the storm appears to be moving faster towards us and threatens to cut us off from our campsite.

Again the eagle swoops, and again floats up to a tall pine ahead of us. As Donny takes more pictures, I suddenly figure out why the eagle is swooping. We've got a stringer of fish hanging off the side of our canoe, and he's looking for dinner.

Eventually we make it back to our bay. We scramble up on a small island to fillet the fish. Sea gulls have found us, and two more eagles show up for dinner. I clean the fish, leaving innards and skin as we head into our campsite while the storm, still to our west, approaches ominously.

We rush to get tarps up over our firewood and food packs as sea gulls, crows and eagles fight over fish guts. The skies dump a deluge of rain on our campsite. We settle in under our tarp while Shane and Steve make dikes around our shelter. The rain doesn't last long, our fire is still going, and our gear and firewood stayed dry. The cool after the rain makes for a pleasant cocktail hour as we watch Greg fix our dinner of fried northern pike.

Saturday morning we break camp, have breakfast and head east to our first portages, a 20-rod and a 4-rod portage into Muskeg Lake. As we approach our next portage to Kiskadinna Lake, I look up the steep wooded slope to the southeast, and I wonder out loud if we have to climb that small mountain to get to the next lake. We do; the 185-rod portage is 95 rods up and 90 rods down-- a real challenge for all, especially the canoe carriers, Greg, Donny, and Steve.

Shane and I trudge on, hoisting our fair share of backpacks. Of course Donny is still hauling the yellow water, although the level is down on both containers. After the small mountain we take it easy and let the west wind blow us eastward on the two-mile stretch of Kiskadinna Lake.

Approaching our next portage, Shane says, "At least this is only 35 rods." Then he glances up at the landing and trail, does a double-take and says, "Whoa!" The trail goes straight up, with footholds chopped into the stiff clay hillside. If it had been raining it would have been like climbing up a waterfall. Our canoe carriers are going to be really tested on this ascent. But working as a team, they hoist the canoes up then down into Omega Lake.

The mile-long paddle to the portage to Winchell Lake refreshes us. With any luck we'll find a campsite on Winchell. We handle this 44-rod portage easily and hope it's our last for the day.

Greg and Donny break away from the portage as soon as we can get them loaded to see if there is still a campsite left. Meanwhile Steve, Shane, and I carry the rest of our gear across the portage, load up, and head out onto the lake.

As the wind gusts from the west, we try to find Greg and Donny in the vastness of the lake. I think I can make them out as we paddle steadily and wearily westward, hoping that they've found a campsite and we won't have to make another portage today. The next lake with campsites is Brule, which is five portages consisting of 323 total rods south.

As we draw closer to the western end of the lake, we spot Greg and Donny unloading at a campsite. What a welcome sight! The campsite is tilted, but we will make it work. After setting up tents and unloading our gear, we settle back. Greg stirs up a meal of salad, rice, chicken, and American fries while Shane and I play War. Donny complains that his shoulder is shot, and he won't be able to carry canoes any further. No sympathy is given.

After dinner we cook popcorn while Shane saws wood. Steve and Donny give directions on where and how the food bag should be elevated from marauding bears. I choose the spot I feel is best. After more than twenty trips into the BWCA and no bear problems, I guess I can make decisions on where and how high to hang the food.

The evening is beautiful with a light breeze out of the southwest. We all take a very refreshing bath in the cool lake because we're all beginning to smell like last month's lunch sitting out in the sun.

We kick back to enjoy the peace and quiet of the beautiful wilderness. Just watching the shadows lengthen on the eastern shore is mesmerizing. Greg is sitting on a rock at the water's edge reading . Donny is still casting from shore looking for the next lunker. Steve is repacking and getting things organized. Shane is cutting wood, eating gummy worms and just enjoying. I'm at peace with world, watching the night overtake the day and reveling in the companionship of my grandson, sons-in-law, and son.

Sunday morning Greg makes pancakes and bacon. We clean up the dishes and break camp with a swiftness we did not have yesterday. We are heading home! Donny's water jugs are a shadow of what they started out to be.

Greg still has surprises left for us, five more portages. We leave camp paddling south to our first portage, a quick, short 14 rods, and we're in Wanihigan Lake heading south. It's only a half mile paddle to our next challenge--our longest portage, 200 rods of mud, downed trees, rocks, and of course a trillion mosquitos. Shane's backpack drops in the mud as we struggle to load the canoes standing in a foot of mud and water swatting mosquitos. Grassy Lake is aptly named, we observe, as we follow the narrow water path.

We have a fairly easy 40-rod portage into Mulligan Lake. As we paddle through Mulligan, we realize that we are going to get a real close up of the devastation left from the storm of '98. The 32-rod portage is cut out of downed and uprooted trees, dislodged car-sized granite boulders. It is almost unbelievable that a wind could tear up 10-foot diameter trees and break them like match sticks. The forest service must have spent a week opening up this portage. We walk through the ravaged landscape with mouths gaping, awestruck by the total destruction.

As we paddle out into Lily Lake we can't help turning around to take another look at the flattened forest. It is amazing what nature can do.

Our last portage, 37 rods long, is anticlimactic. As we traverse the distance in double time, we break out onto Brule Lake still heading south and home. Ahead is a 4-mile paddle to our car.

As we approach our take-out spot, traffic gets pretty heavy with canoes approaching the landing. As we reach the shore, I hop out to back the car up for loading. I shift into reverse, backing towards the landing, when I feel a pull on the wheel. Must be a rut. No, when I get out to look I find the left rear tire flat. Donny and Steve say, "We'll change it." Shane observes and tries to help any way he can. You'd have thought we were at the Indy 500 the way those guys changed that tire.

We finish loading and leave the landing. The drive down the trail is pretty uneventful except for the moose that tries to cross the road. We reflect on a great trip. Shane, Donny and Steve kept up on one of the most grueling trips I've been on in the BWCA. We portaged over 995 rods and paddled more than 24 miles. As we head for home I hope this is the beginning of another fine family tradition.

Burnsville resident Gene Grazzini is a terrazzo, granite, ceramic and marble tile contractor. He has been writing about his hunting and fishing adventures for more than 25 years.

The Storm of the Century
by Verlyn Lane

Before we have another "mega storm" I would like to make an observation about some people who always say, " This could be the storm of the century. " They either have that disease where they don't remember, or they were not old enough to know. The 1936 storm was the worst. The bulk of the snow came in January and February, when it snowed almost every other day, and the snow kept piling up.

Like Wally Schwager, who ran the Legion Club in Blue Earth said, the winter of 1936 was probably the all-time worst in the 20th Century, say nothing about the Armistice Day storm in 1940. Being a bartender, Wally kept up on all such matters that guys talked about when they came to the Legion. All the railroads closed, and the farmers had to cut their fences and come to town with a team and bobsleds.

I lived in Huntley in 1936, and we never had a vehicle in or out of Huntley for two weeks. Snow drifts were six to ten feet high, solid every way you wanted to look. Temperatures never rose above zero for thirty days. The only traffic into town was horse and bobsled. The farmers had paths out in the fields where they could go with horses.

About eight or ten of us kids and young men would walk out to meet the big caterpillar snow plow to break the crust of snow on top so they could push it out a little at a time. Our family milked five or six cows at the time and delivered milk to the teacherage and to about twenty other families in town.

After the big storm, a snow bank about twenty feet tall and forty feet through separated our house from the barn. We had no way of getting the cows out to water and feed, so we built stairs up over this huge snow drift and carried water and feed to them. I never realized cows could eat and drink so much. We pumped all the water by hand into five gallon pails and had to carry them over the drift about a hundred feet to the barn. Our mittens and pants would be frozen solid when we got our chores done.

We milked the cows, then carried the milk to the house for Mom. She would strain it first through the big metal strainer, and then she would strain it through a couple of cloths she had just for that purpose. She would then cool the milk and bottle it. Then my younger brother Avon and I would start out walking with a couple of six-quart crates to deliver our milk. We also had about 25 laying hens so we kept our customers with a good supply of milk and fresh eggs during the two weeks that no supply trucks could get into Huntley.

My good friend Bussy Mikelson and I wished that the town would never be plowed out. I had a little bay Indian pony that we rigged up a light harness for, and we had an old homemade toboggan that we pulled behind the pony. People were running out of coal and other supplies from the store so we ran a delivery service for them. We would get a gunny sack of coal from the elevator, and Bussy would lay over the top of it on the toboggan, and I would ride the pony. We ran errands for the older people and delivered groceries and all sorts of things. We were probably the two richest kids in Huntley at that time. We were making $2 to $3 a day with our service.

We still had plenty of time to play. We would go to Mackies Hill, about a mile or so out of Huntley and go sledding and skating at the creek. We were never idle, and people say that I never changed.

When the plows finally did get through, there was one-lane traffic on most all roads for the remainder of the winter. If you were caught between driveways, someone had to back up for passage.

After all this snow, a terrible hot, dry, windy summer followed. It was the tail wind of all the dust storms of the Dakotas. All in all 1936 was the worst year in the 20th Century as far as I remember.

Verlyn Lane lives in Blue Earth. He sent this story after hearing about Minnesota Memories on Al Malmberg's WCCO late night radio show.

Schooling and Education
by Graham S. Frear

Most people grow nostalgic when talking about early school days, the joys and occasional sorrows or embarrassments of moving from grade to grade in the complex events of acquiring schooling. I differentiate schooling from education; the first is basics, while the second is discovery and mastery of knowledge.

I had grown up from pre- kindergarten through mid fifth grade in a state college laboratory school in central Michigan, where my mother was assistant dean of women, resident head of a large women's dormitory and teacher of home economics. In 1936 we moved back to Minnesota, where my father had been pursuing a Ph.D at the University of Minnesota in the depths of the Great Depression. Mother's work supported his endeavor.

We moved back to Minnesota to live in my grandfather's farm house in Minnetonka Mills, a rural community ten miles west of the Twin Cities. I had experienced an unusual education in the college lab school where every educational innovation and research theory was tried on us and evaluated. I was the object of countless tests and questionnaires, reading tests, verbal skills tests and perceptual problems administered by a succession of coeds enrolled in the elementary education methods courses. I helped build pioneer villages complete with hominy and corn breads, and contributed to countless booklets filled with our stories, poetry and art work. We immersed ourselves in good literature, listened to classical music, went on extended nature hikes and gained exposure to a veritable feast of educational ventures. But we were not firmly grounded in fractions, arithmetic or the mystery of numbers. I knew Michelangelo's David and the Sistine ceiling, could give an oral report on the Vikings and the Icelandic sagas, and in countless sand table panoramas, create a Greek temple, a medieval castle and the pyramids. I knew where the Babylonians built Babel at the confluence of the Tigris and Euphrates long before Iraq became a household name.

My grandfather's house had no indoor plumbing or running water. I was enrolled in a four-room, eight-grade rural elementary school across

the road from our house. I confronted for the first time hard core education that included fractions, geography, civics, science, grammar, spell-
ing, composition and music. I had to be tutored in arithmetic and never
obtained proficiency until I approached graduate work in college.

As a city kid whose parents were college graduates, my first problem in
this rural school in Minnetonka Mills, built on the edge of famous
Minnehaha Creek, was to defend myself from school bullies who considered me prissy and effete. I received numerous bloody noses in recess
altercations, a finger crooked to this day from a bad sprain in a fight, and
numerous abrasions when thrown down on the gravel playground. When
they discovered I could run, play good ball, skate and swing a good softball bat, the fights ceased. I could now bloody a nose with the best.

Each of our four teachers taught two grades. I got the only male teacher,
Mr. Welke, who taught fifth and sixth grade. A superb teacher, he was
particularly good in natural sciences, and he laid out a nature trail in the
heavily wooded area along the creek across from the school. He made
signs identifying by common and taxonomic name all tree species and
patches of perennial wild flowers, including trout lily and yellow mocca-
sin flower. We collected empty bird nests and learned to identify the black-
bird egg from the meadowlark's. We examined creatures in the creek and
brought home fruit jars of polliwogs, water beetles and minnows. We
collected twigs with insect cocoons, scrapbooks of pressed leaves and
wild flowers; we studied the life cycle of the earthworm (lumbricus
terrestris) and had samples of all sedimentary and igneous rocks in our
glacial terrain. We looked for blood red carnelian agates in gravel pits.

Our school had a multi-purpose gym-auditorium-basketball floor-recital
hall-assembly room. We were heated by steam in a substantially well-
built brick building. One large room lined with shelves was a branch of
the Hennepin County Library system, giving us access to magazines, reference books and numerous books for young people and adults, replen-
ished weekly from the book mobile.

Seventh and eighth grade were taught by our spinster principal, a thoroughly grounded teacher and administrator who ran an efficient school

with good faculty. She organized a full program in physical education and organized seasonal play days where we competed for prizes. The school boasted two well-built clay tennis courts, which in winter were flooded for a sizable ice rink. The custodian built a toboggan to slide from the small hill behind the school to the creek in front. Lively hockey games and pull away were daily and nightly events on the ice rink. All of us became proficient tennis players during summers.

One task was acquiring a thorough grounding in academics in preparation for the yearly State Board Tests in English grammar, civics, geography, arithmetic and Minnesota history. Failure in any of these resulted in more course work until you could pass. Our school custodian, a Swedish carpenter, taught the boys shop in a small but well-equipped manual arts program where we built tie racks, knife racks, spice holders, bread boards and bird houses. Girls had classes in cooking and sewing. Our products were always exhibited at the Hennepin County Fair, regardless of sophistication or lack thereof.

Looking back, I am amazed at the quality of education, its stress on fundamentals, and its variety and depth. Our school provided a sound, no-frills education. We had recitals, put on pageants, did plays, had outside assembly speakers and entertainers. We produced an elaborate annual Christmas program and a big music recital in the spring where pianists and singers faced a large audience of peers and parents. Our rural education was a sound, productive experience. How teachers could handle the academics, the arts, music, and take two grades through a full day of courses was a wonder of skill and determination. We never thought of how little they were paid or about their personal lives. All but Mr. Welke were unmarried and lived in homes or apartments in nearby Hopkins.

We were country kids when we graduated to attend Hopkins High School three miles away. There was no bus service in our first two years, and when it came we were the "bus kids" who had to fight for acceptance from the "townies" with their cars and sophisticated girlfriends, the cheerleaders and class secretaries. But we gradually bulldozed our way into sports teams and other activities. We found the townie girls were no different than the country girls. We hung out in the town drug store listening to Glen Miller and Artie Shaw on the jukebox and drinking gallons of frosted malts and cherry Cokes. After games many of us visited out-of-town beer halls to drink bottles of 3.2 beer with no ID required.

Memories of the skating rink, shop, bag lunches at our desks with bottled milk intersperse with those of swimming in gravel pits or the creek, and skiing behind a Model A Ford on a clothes line cable dodging mail boxes. We built complicated tree houses in the high oaks in the woods and stretched long cables down to other trees, then slid down on a sling seat and pulley from the barn. If you did not land on the lower tree with your feet, you risked crashing dangerously into the trunk.

We waged complex western and war games, choosing sides as Germans or Doughboys, Indians or frontiersmen. An abandoned farm with its out buildings provided Dodge City or the Somme. We had cap pistols, rubber guns, BB guns and glow guns made from brass tubing firing dried peas. One missed shot could put an eye out. We went on moonlight ski trips and had huge cookouts until early morning on wooded hilltops. The windmill tower provided us with a crow's nest on the *Bounty* or *Constitution.*

We suffered through an early awareness of sexuality, but knew nothing of French kissing, condoms, oral sex or pornography. We flipped up girls' skirts and yelled, "I see London, I see France, I see Lizzie's underpants." We suffered through the embarrassment of an unexpected erection while giving a book report in front of the group. But we weathered the travails, and most of us matured, married and raised children of our own.

We received a no-frills, basic education taught by dedicated teachers. We survived without VCRs, computers, cell phones, TV, compact discs, and "Saturday Night Live." We developed sound minds in our four-room brick school, and sound bodies in the land around it. Our world functioned dynamically and positively. We were a fortunate generation. Our kind will not come this way again. We were truly blessed. Sixty-four years later, I still have my tie rack and a small book of poetry given by the principal for winning top honors in the state board geography exam. I was paid dividends to read *National Geographic* maps.

Graham Frear is a retired St. Olaf English and Irish studies professor.

After High School, 1947
By Lloyd Deuel

After I graduated from high school, I was uncertain about my career goals so I stayed around my home town of Foreston and tried a few jobs. In the fall of 1947, Ernie and Earl Axt asked me to come to work shoveling gravel. These brothers were my dad's cousins, and I had known them all my life. They had a gravel hauling business, and they owned a 1936 Diamond T dump truck. Unlike most dump trucks in those days, this one had a 4-yard dump box instead of a 3-yard box. This truck had mechanical brakes, which was almost like no brakes, and of course no power steering.

We loaded gravel out of Al Bemis' gravel pit located near the Estes Brook General Store in Mille Lacs County. The Axt Brothers were to introduce a loader the following year, but there was no mechanical loader in the pit when I worked there. This meant I had to shovel gravel into the truck with long-handle Number 2 shovels. They had a lot of gravel orders to fill, and one more shoveler would mean extra loads each day. After loading the truck, we would get a break by riding to where it was dumped by the truck's hydraulic dumping system. Ernie and Earl Axt had been doing road construction for 20 years before I was born and were highly seasoned shovelers. It took extra effort on my part to match them shovel for shovel without pause, but I was young and strong. They paid me 50 cents per hour for this work.

Also hauling out of the Bemis pit were Curtis and Dale Siemers. I had known them all my life, and we exchanged friendly insults.. They had an older truck with a wooden platform box with 12 inch wooden sides. This truck had no hydraulic dumping system, which meant they had to unload gravel off by hand. They shoveled with long-handled flat-bottom shovels that were used in grain elevators and feed stores, and I think they were called "millers' shovels." It required supreme effort to shovel gravel with those shovels. Nevertheless, the Siemers seemed to match us nonstop, with no break in rhythm. The Axt Brothers said that the flat bottoms were better for unloading, but they really needed the Number 2 shovels for loading. The Siemers Brothers operated a no-frill gravel hauling business, and there was no room in their low budget for a couple extra shovels.

After the Axt Brothers caught up on their gravel hauling, I went to work plowing for Ardis Hoversten on his farm near Foreston. I used his Model B John Deere tractor pulling a 2-bottom plow. This was a good plowing fall, and I plowed a 36-acre field in six days, which pleased Ardis so much he kept me working with his other fields afterwards. He also had me driving his dad's borrowed truck hauling corn from southern Minnesota for his feeder hog operation.

Ardis had about 45 steers that he kept at his brother Ray Hoversten's farm in Benton County. He asked me to come to work early one morning because he was shipping the steers to market at South St. Paul, and we had to get them ready to be loaded. He explained that he was going to hire Hewart Siemers as his hauler because Hewart would come early with three trucks and load all the steers and haul them to market.

It was still dark when Ardis and I fed and watered the steers. At 7 a.m. Hewart Siemers drove into the yard in his car with his three youngest sons, Sheldon, Bill, and Bob. His next three sons, Wayne, Curtis, and Dale followed into the yard with each driving a clean, late model cattle truck. Wayne, the oldest, was my age--18 years old. The Siemer boys outnumbered me, and I had to endure questions like, "What's a big city (Foreston) boy like you doing out of bed this early in the morning?"

There were already cattle in the trucks, which meant that they had already gone out to other farms and picked up quite a few before coming for these steers. I had never seen cattle loaded into trucks before and didn't quite know what was expected of me. It turned out to be nothing at all, and I joined Ardis and Hewart on the sidelines. These guys knew exactly how to go about loading cattle, and even the three younger brothers knew what was expected of them.

There was no lost motion in the entire operation, but the three younger boys got yelled at a lot by their older brothers. By 8 the loading was done, and the three older brothers drove away headed for the South St Paul stockyards. Hewart left to drop his three younger sons off at school, and since he was the Benton County Sheriff, he headed for his office in the Foley courthouse.

I worked for Ardis for a month doing his plowing and fall work. He surprised me by paying more than the expected 50 cents per hour. I discovered that I had severe allergies, so farm work could not be my vocation.

After the farm work was over for the fall we had a severe snowstorm late in November. Ardis' wife Leola had a baby boy in Milaca, and as he set out to pick up his wife and son at the hospital, Ardis got his pickup stuck in the snow before he left his yard. He called my dad, Ira Deuel, and asked if we would go to town with Dad's car and meet Ardis with his John Deere tractor halfway on the road. Snowplowed roads in 1947 were hit and miss and unreliable. We picked up mother and baby and got back to where the tractor was parked, and then I drove the tractor while Dad and Ardis took the baby and his mother home. I had to pull Ardis' pickup loose from the snow, and then get both pickup and tractor into the garage. My dad and I were able to get his car through the snow and home.

In January of 1948, I was asked to be part of an ice harvesting crew. Art Harstad had bought my parents' restaurant tavern and needed the ice house filled. We didn't have electric coolers, and cooling was done by ice. I had been the "iceman" in town and had experience handling ice. My dad had taught me how not to manhandle cakes of ice, but rather use "finesse," and that's why I was asked to be part of the crew. The others were Donald Kennedy, Jack Buisman, and his son Don, who was my buddy. Kennedy and Jack received $1 per hour while Don and I made 75 cents.

Ernie and Earl Axt had always had the contracts to fill icehouses in the winter, but they declined this job and allowed us to borrow their equipment. The equipment consisted of a 60" circular saw blade mounted on a pull-by-hand sled powered by a gas engine. They also supplied ice tongs, pulleys, ice chisel, walkers to clamp on our feet to prevent slipping into the water, and a ramp to load ice cakes from the truck up into the icehouse.

The weather had been bitter cold, and we decided we wouldn't start if the temperature on the Foreston Oil Company's big thermometer registered colder than minus 20 and the wind velocity, according to the St. Cloud radio station, was stronger than 25 miles per hour.

We were to cut ice on the L.K. Nelson gravel pit. This pit was started by the railroad, but then they hit an underground spring, and the pit filled with crystal clear clean water. Our one unexpected break was that the snow had been blown off the ice where we were planning to cut so we didn't have to shovel snow before sawing ice.

We selected a spot and started sawing first a one-direction grid and then a second grid at square crossways. We got the hang of this quickly after getting the gas engine started. Next we had to chop a couple cakes and waste them to make room to get the rest out of the water. The saw only cut about 24" through 42" thick ice cakes, but a blow with a chisel made them break cleanly. We cut footholds for two us next to the hole, clamped the tongs onto the floating cake, did a one-two and yanked the cake out.

The cake would come out with a water splash onto our pants legs. This did not bother us because our pants froze stiff. We were more concerned about slipping into the water, but nobody did. We changed positions often, kept our mittens dry, and made sure there were no signs of frostbite on anyone. The weather never warmed to more than -15, and the wind was constantly blowing. There were days when the temperature would hit nearly -40, and we did not attempt work.

When we had enough for a few truckloads, we used the ramp and slid ice cakes, which weighed about 400 pounds each, onto the truck. We then started to fill the icehouse. The cakes moved easily once they were started, and the trick was to keep each ice cake moving until in place. We left about a 10 inch gap between the rows of ice and the outside walls.. Don and I were to shovel sawdust for insulation onto the tops and down the sides before spring.

When I went home for lunch my pants were frozen stiff, and when I attempted to sit down it felt like my legs were encased in oversized stovepipes. I ate in the standing position, and inside the house my pants started to thaw and the cold started coming through. It felt better to stay outside as much as possible. The daylight hours were short, and we had to quit early. I walked home stiff legged. My pants felt like boards, and my parents had to help me get them off. That was when cold seeped into me, and I spent time in the hot bathtub just warming up.

We had left some cut cakes on the ice the day before, and we wondered how we could get them loose. It turned out to be no problem when we hit their undersides with chisels so we decided to cut cakes and store enough on top for many days of hauling so we wouldn't have to get wet every day.

After loading up the first load, Don started the truck. Crace's 1940 Ford was in good shape, but it had what was called a high-speed transmission that was intended for higher speed on the highway. The first gear was about as fast as second gear in most trucks. To start with a heavy load, the driver had to accelerate quite a bit or the engine would kill. Don was used to this quirk. What he wasn't expecting was that he was on very slick ice so the wheels spun. When the wheels suddenly grabbed, the truck lurched in the direction the front wheels were pointing. This caused the truck to spin around counterclockwise about three or four times in what seemed like the blink of an eye.

The cakes of ice spit off the truck like popping popcorn in a kettle with no lid. It seemed like they picked up speed after they had traveled a ways on the ice. There were 400 lb. ice cakes traveling in all direction. They kept going until they came to the banks where some would tumble over the top. Others crashed into the rows of ice we had positioned for later loading and just exploded.

Fortunately we were behind the rows of ice to be loaded. The saw, sled and all the equipment were safely back with us. There was no damage, but we had to reload the truck. There was a lot to be said, and there was a lot said. We got the icehouse filled, and it was a very neat job. Art Harstad was pleased, and we had just finished when the snows of 1948 hit with about the biggest snowfall in years.

When young men did this kind of work, the modern disease called teen-age obesity was unheard of. However, with gravel shoveling, plowing, trucking, cattle rustling, rescuing winter travelers and ice harvesting under my belt, I decided to try for a vocation that required inside work.

Lloyd Deuel is a retired machinist in Brooklyn Center who enjoys woodworking, reading and cribbage. He and his wife Phyllis enjoy gardening.

Lost Trains in a Cocoon of Snow
by Ken Kelly as relayed by his father, Roy N. Kelly

During the winter of 1912, a savage storm unleashed itself and swept out of the western sky across Minnesota, engulfing everything in billowy white. Winter had come upon the wild prairies of Minnesota with a rampaging fury, dumping huge piles of snow across the barren land.

The frolicking wind scrawled myriads of wavy lines across dazzling snowfields, broadcasting tiny folds of undulating valleys and diamond-studded hills as far as the eye could see. A shimmering sea of ice gems gave pleasure to the enchanted eye. A vast no-man's land of glittering, rolling fluffy prairie seemed to stretch to the edge of the world and disappear into a vast unknown abyss as frosty crystals spewed into the air.

In the midst of this savage storm, I was called by the yardmaster to be conductor on Time Freight #61 to go west from Austin headed for Jackson. My engineer was to be Joe Lorenze. We were to move a heavy train of 45 boxcars carrying 1800 tons. Before we left the Austin switching yards, the tramp switch engine and crew coupled a plow onto our engine. The 7 a.m. lead engine and crew at the south end of the yards coupled a flanger on our caboose. The flanger would cut the impacted snow and ice from between the rails and eliminate the danger of derailing other trains that would follow in our tracks.

Passenger Train #203, pushing a snow plow, had left Austin 72 hours ahead of us. They became stuck in the wild storm somewhere after leaving Fairmont and had not arrived at Jackson. The train dispatcher was unable to pinpoint their exact location, but they were lost within an area of 30 miles. Our running orders were to proceed with extreme caution after departing Fairmont.

As we proceeded west, we found the lost trains snared by a cocoon of snow isolated and swallowed up by the tumultuous storm. They were located in a hollow between Sherburne and Alpha about 90 miles west of Austin, and their crews desperately needed assistance and relief. The temperature had dropped to -10 with strong winds out of the northwest. Passenger Train #203 was lost in a drift 20 feet deep and 1000 feet long.

Also in this drift was a snowplow with engine and caboose wrapped tightly in blown snow. The cab of the engine was blown full of powdered snow. The crew had killed the fire in the firebox of the engine to keep it from blowing up and had then retreated to the caboose. The gauge had indicated a dangerously low water supply to provide steam power for the locomotive, and the crew had provided for their survival by moving coal from the coal tender to the caboose.

I had previously seen a blown and gutted engine, and it was not a pretty sight with its boiler split asunder, wrenched innards lying haphazardly around, ruins of framework lying in grotesquely jangled fashion and wheels and axle lying one atop the other or standing on end. With skeletal boiler staves bent and twisted, water tank burst open at the seams, coal tender split asunder, and unrecognizable parts strewn over a wide area, the heavy iron frame looks like a turkey after it's been picked clean. We wanted to prevent such a disaster from overtaking Train #203.

When fully operational, the silent sleeping engine, with hot water flowing through its copper veins and steam escaping from its cylinder cock nostrils of steel, can pull many times its own weight over long distances. But now this train was helpless as it was engulfed in winter's icy grasp.

It was hard to comprehend the savage force of this storm. I knew that the snowplow due out of Jackson was supposed to have an L-2 class engine with power to spare. It was supposed to be big enough to take on most drifts, but not the magnitude of the drift that had captured these two trains.   No ordinary engine and plow could free them. It would take a rotary plow from the Cascade Mountains area of Oregon that could eat snow and spit it out the side in one continuous, smooth-flowing action.

Unknown to us, the Jackson crew had encountered a problem. Snow had plugged the Jackson turntable and kept the L-2 class engine out of service. The Jackson crew had to wait for a G-8 class engine to arrive from Madison, South Dakota. When that engine arrived, it was refueled with a tender full of coal, and its water tank was topped to overflowing. In a race against time, that snowplow with full crew left Jackson going east to clear the main line of all drifts. Its conductor and engineer were given authority over all first class trains. Their running orders were to hurry and find the lost trains and give needed assistance. The stranded plow and engine were somewhere between Jackson and Fairmont, but unknown to the conductor and engineer, the lost train wasn't protected by a flagman.

I sat in the caboose of Freight #61, which swayed as we traveled west, enjoying the warmth of the fire in its pot-bellied stove. As I gazed out the window that had a lacy pattern painted by Jack Frost, I wished I had a camera to capture the magnitude and beauty of the storm. But the cozy warmth of the caboose belied the stark reality of the outside weather. Since I had walked to work that morning, I had already tasted what was to come.

Our train came to a halt after two torpedoes placed on the rails warned us with a loud bang bang that another train was just ahead. My brother, a brakeman on #203, had taken flagging equipment and walked a half mile east to protect passengers and train #203 from our approach from the rear.

I took a pair of heavy wool socks from my pocket and slipped them on over my shoes to insulate my feet from the cold. I knew the hours ahead would be long and demanding with little letup in the work. To fortify myself, I then slapped on my buckle-up overshoes with their thin flannel lining. I wrapped a long wool scarf around my neck, put on my Mackinaw jacket, and fastened all the buttons to keep out the cold. I put on my deerskin chopper mitts with wool liners.

I took a deep breath and stepped outside into the frigid fingers of air that penetrated my body. The first blast of cold almost took my breath away, but with great effort I made my way from my caboose to my steam engine. My brother met me and told me what the situation was up ahead. We climbed up into the cab of my locomotive and proceeded to within 50 feet of his stalled train.

In my wildest imagination I couldn't have foreseen this huge, white cocoon. I wasn't prepared for this amazing sight, but I thought it was imperative to get everyone transferred to our engine from the passenger train so we could get them to Fairmont as quickly as possible for food and rest.

I went into the hind coach and told everyone we would shuttle all to Fairmont. There was an engine crew, a train crew, a baggage man, and a mail clerk, eighteen passengers and a drummer who rode the rails trying to eke out a living selling apples, gum, candy, sandwiches, and the *Chicago Daily Blade*.

A total of 28 people crowded into the cab of our locomotive. I told my engineer and brakeman to shuttle everyone to Fairmont, leave our train on the main line after cutting the crossings, and whistle out a flagman to protect our train from the rear. The hind brakeman was to go back a half mile, place two torpedoes 100 feet apart, and then return to the caboose to have necessary equipment ready to flag down any approaching train. Any train hitting those two torpedoes was warned to reduce speed and be ready to halt. I then told the head brakeman and engineer to return to the stalled train and wait for word from me. I left my crew to their own devices to carry out my orders.

People were packed into the cab of our engine like ten pounds of spuds in a five-pound bag. Our engine was about nine feet by seven, and we opened a curtain on the coal tender to add another five feet. People even squeezed into a confined space by the boiler head, the warmest spot of all. They were thankful to be going back to Fairmont after being stranded for almost three days in the howling snowstorm.

I told the engineer to wait for a signal from me to let them know I made it to the far end of the huge drift, and then they were to proceed back to Fairmont and discharge their duties. The stillness of the frozen prairie was almost maddening. Only the rhythmical pulsating of our workhorse broke the silence with its thump, thump, thump.

Swirling, piercing snow clawed at my clothes and face as I traversed the monstrous 1000-foot drift to the west to see what was being done there to alleviate the predicament of the stalled train. The storm had abated, but the swirling 25-mile-per-hour winds lashed out as I made my way. My breathing was heavy and rapid, and the icy air burned my lungs. I hid my face in the scarf that was encrusted with ice crystals from the vapor of my breath. I had never been so cold, and sundogs, streaking showers of bright light on either side of the sun, attested to the bitter conditions.

My love of railroading and my anticipation of the day's events kept me going. I never tired of what I was doing. It was a day God made, and I was going to make the most of it. My cardinal rule was that it could be as good as the best and better than most. I loved what I was doing.

I glanced skyward, and the sky was breathtakingly ice blue. The vast awesome space sent a shiver through my body. I labored so hard I was actually sweating, and my long johns were cold and clammy on my back. As a cold chill scampered up and down my spine, I became mesmerized by the whiteout. I had no depth perception, and distance was nonexistent.

I became exhausted and turned my back to the howling winds. I took deep breaths and looked back at the smoke from my engine that swirled down against the white snow in startling contrast. Flecks of sooty cinders from the smokestack of the workhorse etched lines in the white snow.

I figured that I had come about 500 feet, and I asked myself what I was doing out here. People who worked in offices were lucky. I thought about the warm caboose I left and settled myself against what lay ahead.

Mixed emotions of fear and excitement overcame me for a second, but I forged ahead. I slapped my hands together as my fingertips tingled from the cold. Tears came to my eyes and made it difficult to see. I kept wiping my eye with my coat sleeve for better vision.

As I looked west, my heart leaped with pangs of excitement and exhilaration. Black smoke on the horizon was the key to what was coming. The plow from Jackson was on the lookout for the trains that had been swallowed by the storm. I turned for a brief respite to catch my breath and gazed at my engine's black smoke. Then fear grabbed me, and I whirled and looked at the smoke from the engine and plow bearing straight down at us. I felt completely helpless and frightened and wanted to go in nine directions at once. My heart raced, and my mind reeled with anxiety.

As I turned, I stumbled and fell. Scrambling to my feet, I plunged ahead and soon saw the tip of the caboose stovepipe protruding from the snow with gray smoke puffs escaping into the wild winds.

I found gandy dancers, a name given to men who lay rail and tie and bind them to roadbeds. They were shoveling snow, cleaning out around the caboose wheels. I hollered, "Get the hell out of there!" and they dropped their shovels and came out of the deep cavernous hole like blackbirds scattering out of a briar patch.

I slid down the steep bank of snow onto the caboose steps and tore open the door. I hollered to the crew, "Is there a flagman out?" When they said no, I grabbed a fusee from the overhead rack and yelled, "You jackasses, a plow's heading straight at you. Run for it!"

I scrambled outside and clawed my way up the ladder to the top of the caboose. I popped the tie-down tape from the end of the fusee and struck the explosive ends together. The fusee burst into life with bright red flame and yellow ghostly smoke spewing from it. I got a whiff of the sulfur smell, waved the fusee once, and a gust of wind snuffed out the light. "Damn," I yelled and threw it towards the rightaway. I grabbed my Scotch cap from my head and swung my arms wildly.

The engine rushed toward us with snow cascading around the cab of the frost-coated engine. It was a complete whiteout with zero visibility looking from inside the cab through a small window to the front of the engine. The engineer, running blind, thought the smoke from my engine was the lost train. He was unaware of the two lost trains just in front of him.

I shouted "Plug her! Put her in the big hole, Stop," but the wild winds drowned out my voice. I could hardly hear myself shouting, but as if he anticipated my warning, the engineer on the plow from Jackson slid open his side window to peer out. He froze with his hand at the throttle as terror gripped him. He put her in the big hole, applying all the braking power at his command to the G-8 workhorse, but it was too late. He was already upon the huge drift and trains that lay motionless and cold in his path.

Wild thoughts flashed through my half-frozen mind. How many of us would lose our lives to the stupidity of one man who hadn't sent out a flagman? I was mad as hell. Thoughts flashed before me with blazing speed as I tried to save myself.

Just a few seconds before the engine hit the huge drift, I flung myself away down the steep drift, rolling away as fast as I could. Fearful that my life would be snuffed out like the fusee in the wind, I almost could feel the cold, cutting knife-blade of the snowplow sear and tear into my warm body. When I stopped rolling down the incline I was elated, delirious with joy, to be in one piece.

The thump-thump-thump of the engine on the plow brought me to my feet in a hurry. The engine had pushed its plow off the track, and the plow lay at a crazy angle. It had smashed the corner of the caboose as it left the rails climbing and skidding up the bank of crusted snow. I hurried to the engineer, who told me what I had already surmised; he thought the smoke from my engine was the lost trains.

How glad I was that it was a G-8 engine, slow and ponderous, hitting those drifts at 15 miles per hour. If it had been the L-2 class engine, it would have been there sooner, and God only knows how many men would have lost their lives. I think God played a hand in plugging the turntable with snow at Jackson. How glad I was to be able to reach the caboose and warn all those men to flee to safety. With a more powerful and speedy engine, death would have been a breath away.

Roy Kelly worked for the railroad for 53 years, and his son, Ken Kelly, worked for the Chicago, Milwaukee, St. Paul Pacific for 25 years. Now retired in Austin with his wife Elnora, Ken enjoys writing poetry.

Roy Kelly, conductor in this story.

Your Real Name is...
by Carol Keech Malzahn

Until I was almost 6 years old, I didn't believe I was actually related to any of my brothers, sisters, or even my parents. I believed, in my own little child's mind, that I was adopted. I was the only one in the family with bright red hair. I always wanted to say it was orange. It was a far cry from the color red in my opinion, and it was my most significant feature, besides my freckles and the fact that I was a little smaller than most girls my age. The combination of those three characteristics created a huge focus of attention. I asked for and loved some of this attention, but I assuredly did not appreciate most of it.

Along with red hair, freckles and small size came a book full of nick-names. The name that stuck and that everyone called me from as far back as I could remember was Teeny. I didn't question it or mind it too much until a new neighbor lady named Emma, who also happened to have red hair that came out of a bottle, moved in with a dog named Tiny, who also had red hair.

We lived near a small hamlet named Sveadahl, northwest of St. James. The church, store, and the station were the hubs of our daily social lives. Emma and her husband Kenny owned the station. Tiny, the dog, was in the station whenever we stopped in and was known by everyone who lived within twenty miles of Sveadahl. Back in the 1960s, that was a fair number of people.

Often people would get my name, Teeny, mixed up with the dog's name and call me Tiny, then Teeny, then Tiny again, then walk away throwing up their hands. I would be embarrassed to no end, and I could never hide my embarrassment as my face turned bright red from blushing.

My older brother John would pick up on this and start to tease me and whistle, "Tiny, here Tiny... Can you speak? ... roll over?? .... sit???" It was a great joke on me!

I started to wonder what my mother was thinking when she named me Teeny. My other siblings were named William, Sharon, and John; then I came along and she came up with Teeny? Even my younger sister Kathleen, who was born after me, had a regular name. What had possessed my mother on the day I was born, May 24,1954, was more than I could begin to imagine. Teeny… how ridiculous. I grew to HATE that name and resent my mother for naming me that. I certainly had to have been adopted.

It was a hot summer day, and Roger Olson, the handsome, older neighbor boy, drove into the yard to drop off Sharon, my older sister. I think she had been at baton twirling lessons with Roger's sister. Anyway, I stopped what I was doing to get a look at Roger and wave at the girls in the car. Roger hollered out the car window at me, "Hi Tiny!"

John heard it and started teasing me. I was mortified. John's friends, Gene Lindquist and Dean Siem were also there. They all started taunting me, "Speak….roll over….sit…..want your tummy patted????" The girls were all laughing at me too. It was more than I could bear.

I started crying and yelling at them to stop teasing me. The madder I got, the more fun they had! Finally, in deepest humiliation, I went storming into the house to Mother. "This is all your fault! Why did you ever give me such a stupid name as Teeny?"

As Mom picked me up and set me on her lap and started rubbing my back, I could not stop the tears. She said, "We did not name you Teeny. That is just your nickname." I was totally astounded. One thought ran through my head. How bad is my real name if they started calling me such a terrible nickname? "Your real name is Carol".

I could barely believe my ears. "Carol. Carol." I had to say it a couple of times. It felt very strange.

I wasn't immediately impressed, but it was sure a lot better than Teeny. I actually had a nice, grown-up name. My next challenge was, of course, figuring out how to get everyone to stop calling me Teeny.

I asked Mom, and she told me the story about her sister, Aunt Violet Parker. Her nickname was Toots. (We were never told why until we were old enough to figure it out on our own!) Everyone called her Toots until one day she got really mad and yelled at everyone to stop calling her by her nickname and call her by her real name, Violet. So I went marching back outside and yelled at those boys to stop calling me by my nickname and to call me by my real name Carol. I remember John being a little surprised. Maybe he didn't know my real name either.

Of course it didn't take long… "Christmas Carol! Christmas Carol!" John shouted out. It just didn't get the same results. Everybody calls me Carol now. I am no longer called Teeny, except by my loving brothers and sisters on special occasions.

Carol grew up on a farm near Sveadahl (between St. James and Comfrey). A job drew her to Minnesota Lake, where she met her husband Art, raised two children and lives happily ever after.

Teeny, age 4

To Mr. Blackmur, with Gratitude
by Nancy Smiler Levinson

I am sitting in my tenth grade English class at Washburn High School in Minneapolis. The year is 1952. It is a still, white, winter day. Outside the windows are frosted. Inside the radiators crackle and hiss. Mr. Blackmur, the teacher, a tall, dark-haired man who speaks with a gentle, dramatic flair, opens discussion of an assigned story, Jack London's "To Build a Fire," about a man in the Yukon who ignores the advice of old timers and ventures out alone into dangerously cold weather.

"How does the author build tension?" the teacher asks. "What details help you feel the increasing cold? What is the relationship between the man and his dog? Does the man have a name? Why not? What is the author telling us? What is this story really about?"

I sit captivated, interested not only in the character who fails in his attempts to build a fire to survive and soon freezes to death, but also much caught up with the exploration and exchange that Mr. Blackmur elicits. Who had considered that so many thoughtful questions could be pulled from so short a story?

When the bell rings, I am startled. All around the classroom books are gathered, chairs scrape over the floor, feet shuffle . . . it takes a minute for me to shake myself back from the Yukon where man has lost his struggle against nature. Only then do I hear the teacher calling my name. "Nancy Smiler, do you want to stop by after the last bell today?"

Because I mentioned to him that I am trying to write fiction, Mr. Blackmur has kindly offered to look at whatever I am willing to share. He has read my story, "The Dance," about a girl having a dreamy evening at a prom who drops a crystal punch glass—only to have it suddenly revealed that the glass is a kitchen tumbler that shatters in the sink because she is actually at home washing dishes, imagining herself awhirl at the dance.

Mr. Blackmur tells me he likes the story and the surprise ending. He also tells me he likes "the sensibility of the girl, who is open and forthcoming about her loneliness and desire to belong." With this he gives me permission, encourages me, to express personal, deep feelings on paper. How remarkable! Then he says, "Keep on writing," and I know that I will.

Throughout the year I share other stories with him, and he continues to praise me and urge me on. Sometimes he suggests I read a story or novel that relates to a subject or new style that I have tried so I can see how another author handles characterization or dialogue or theme.

Looking back, I blush with embarrassment at my adolescent angst, and worse, at some really bad writing. Having no one else with whom I could truly share writing experiences, his support and sensibilities long carried me. After my high school graduation ceremony on the football field, I searched the crowd for him so that I could say goodbye and thanks. I didn't fully realize that day how many thanks I owed him.

Forty-five years have passed. I have lived and worked in New York and now live in southern California. It has been my good fortune to have written and published a stream of books for young readers, including fiction, historical fiction, biographies, and history, as well as dozens of stories for magazines and a children's page in the *Los Angeles Times*. Not without challenge and struggle, of course, I might add.

It is a hot Sunday afternoon in June of 2001. I am visiting my hometown on a weekend of an all-school reunion and have stopped by the high school. Crowds are wandering, peering into past homerooms, the gym, the auditorium, the library (now media center). . .outside the principal and city mayor are speech-making.

I overhear that the English teacher Robert Blackmur is around somewhere, wearing sunglasses and a blue baseball cap. I search for him at once, and when I find him, I ask to be sure, "Mr. Blackmur?" "Yes, I am," he acknowledges. In an emotional outburst, I throw my arms around him. He is taken aback by this stranger. Of course he has no idea who I am. I step away, catch my breath, and tell him who I am and how happy I am to see him again.

He is incredulous at hearing of my work and his role of influence. He asks question after question about me and my writing life, listening attentively to every response.

Finally, thinking that he looks very well-preserved for a retired teacher, I remark lightheartedly, "You were so much older in class, but it seems now I have caught up with you in age."

"I'm 72," he answers, smiling. It turns out that he is only ten years older than I am. What I had thought to be a wise, seasoned teacher was a young man in his mid-20s, beginning his career.

We exchange cards and email addresses. I send him an author brochure and three of my titles, a biography, a middle grade novel, and an easy-to-read historical fiction.

A letter from him arrives, genuinely thanking me for each book and kindly noting something specific and rewarding about each, while also commenting with delight on my "enthusiastic" meeting with him at the reunion. Mr. Blackmur signs off with, "Profound admiration and gratitude, Bob." Bob!

The letter is so generous with compliments that I blush while reading it. It's clear that he took time and effort crafting it. He is, after all, still the model and caring teacher. "Mentor" was not a word in popular use back in the '50s, but certainly Bob, in welcoming me in from the cold, was just that. How grateful I am meeting up with him decades later so that I could tell him so.

Los Angeles resident Nancy Smiler Levinson, a native of Minneapolis, is author of 26 books for young readers and numerous magazine and newspaper stories.

Nancy Smiler, 1954.

Alvera E. Lustig, Our Mom
by Marilyn F. Lustig and Rosalie A. Schnick

The Olp Sisters. This phrase had meaning for many people near Deerfield in the early part of the Twentieth Century—six girls, all so very strong and unique. Now they are all gone, but their children and grandchildren remain to carry on.

Mom, the youngest sister, was a young adult during the Great Depression, which affected her greatly. She was bright and wanted to have a business career. Fate did not allow that to happen, but fate brought Mom and Dad together at a dance. They had come to the dance with others, but they left together. Their marriage began in 1939 and lasted 62 years.

One of Mom's favorite memories was of their honeymoon driving in their Model A across dirt roads and riding a raft on the Missouri River to Montana to visit friends. Mom loved western movies, particularly Gene Autry, so that trip was special. When they returned they lived in an old house without electricity or central heat outside Owatonna. She lived in that house for four years, gave birth to two children, and survived.

They moved to another farm house, where Mom proved her industry by butchering hogs and chickens, canning meat, and making sauerkraut, sausage, head cheese and soap. In 1947 her oldest child David was killed by a truck as he was getting off the school bus. Mom was devastated, but she survived. Two more children came along, and Mom ended up with four beautiful children.

Each of us children had our rituals with Mom. All of us went to the store with her list, with the main "grocery" item being cookies. We knew exactly which ones she had to have. She gave us the cash. When we returned, she made sure we got everything on that list, and it was essential that we gave her the receipt so she could check it.

Mom excelled at making preserves, baking pies, cookies, white bread and cakes and canning stewed tomatoes, tomato juice, and ketchup (my favorites). Every year she would take these goodies to the Steele County

Free Fair and win ribbons, many of them blue. There was a gentle rivalry between Mom and her sister Emma Williams over who could get the most ribbons.

Most days the kitchen was where you would find Mom. The great aromas meant Mom was cooking or baking something special. She always wore an apron--just made for children to tug on. For each of our birthdays, Mom would make our favorite cake. Then she would take a picture of the cake and then a picture of us holding the cake or standing by it. And on several occasions during the year, she would make gingerbread men with either raisins or chocolate chips (our brother's favorite). Mom made the best cinnamon and caramel rolls and something she called crispies.

Mom put together picture albums for each of us kids, and when we left home, she did scrapbooks of our high school classmates—their marriages, divorces, and successes. She delighted in hiding Easter eggs throughout the house, putting money under our pillows when we lost our baby teeth, and getting special presents for us at Christmas time. My best memory was my first bicycle, a brand new one. I can still remember the smell of the new tires.

Mom loved to read to us children. I remember her reading *Gone with the Wind* to us. She gave us that wonderful love of reading that we have to this day. Music was also a major part of her life, especially that connected with "old time" hymns and Marilyn's violin playing. Mom listened to church services on the radio every Sunday for the message and for the music. Her church and her religion were very important.

My main ritual with Mom was providing her with an endless supply of 1950s and 60s romance paperbacks, which she loved and read and reread. I would run into the second hand bookstore and gather up ten to fifteen books in five minutes, just by looking at the spines and knowing some authors. The key was that the cover price needed to be 95 cents or less. This indicated that these were older titles and less racy. I would quickly check to see if Mom's markings were inside the front cover and not buy those. Mom would delight in handling each book and remarking on each title.

She kept an extensive notebook of the titles she had read, and she would evaluate each book. Her system was simple: "V.V.Good" for very very good, " V.G, " " Good," or "Do not read again." Sometimes she would also write, "Was V.G. Now V.V.G."

Mom never learned to drive so my dad, our neighbors and we kids drove her to various activities. After Dad died and she moved to Park Place in Owatonna, she used and appreciated the services of Healthy Seniors. She thought it was special when the drivers would wait for her during a doctor's appointment. Healthy Seniors had many requests from Mom for such things as shopping trips, accompanying her to the bank, a class reunion, attending a grief support group, and providing rides to church, clinic, grocery store, and hair salon. One time Healthy Seniors staff member Sara Aeikens took her to the bank to get dimes to play Bingo.

She was the happiest we had known her to be at Park Place the last two and a half years of her life. She would regularly call us up to thank us for finding this wonderful place. She loved the view from her living room window, especially in the fall when leaves changed colors. The staff and residents made her life more full.

She had a sense of humor. She enjoyed telling us about getting her flu shot. She wrote, "The first question they asked me was, ' Are you allergic to eggs?' And I told them I wasn't, and the second questions was, 'Are you pregnant?' No of course not! Imagine, if at 88 years old I should be pregnant."

She loved to play Bingo. As we were looking through the apartment after her stroke, we found numerous pieces of paper with, "I won two games of Bingo, November 20, 2003, $3.20." We children supplied her with jigsaw puzzles, and she would have several going at once. And of course, every time we visited, we would play "Kings in the Corner" with her, and she would regularly win.

The last two weeks of Mom's life were a sacred journey for all of us, a privilege and an honor. In the hospital after Mom's severe stroke on December 21, Pastor Griebel got his hymnal, and we sang Mom's favorite hymns and Christmas carols to her. We could tell she was trying to sing along. We read Psalms and said prayers alone with her, together as a family and often with Pastor Griebel. It was wonderful and so comforting. I played my violin for her for hours, all her favorite hymns and Christmas music. We played audio cassettes of Christmas music, polkas/waltzes and finally Tennessee Ernie Ford singing all those great hymns. Music is healing and transforming.

Mom had a great send-off. As she breathed her last breath of life here on earth, she was surrounded by her family singing "Rock of Ages" and with our sister Charlene on the phone from Phoenix. What a beautiful and peaceful way to leave this earth.

I want to end with one of Mom's favorite words. "Evidentually" was her own unique word. It is a combination of "eventually" and "evidently," and she used it often. God bless you Mom, and evidentually we will all be with you again someday.

Alvera Lustig

Marilyn Lustig, a Minneapolis librarian for 23 years, appreciates the power of the written word. Rosalie (Roz) Schnick, who lives in LaCrosse, is National Coordinator for Aquaculture New Animal Drug Applications, a position she's held for nine years.

Tracking Potter's Prose
by Suzanne Nielsen

I was a train...And the world was my rails... ---Buzz Potter

Reading the obits is my pastime; it's the one way of staying in the know about deaths without having to attend any class or family reunions. Occasionally I shed a moment of sorrow, most often for the kindred spirits I wish I'd known. Such was the case when I read the obits on March 15. Although Trudi Hahn's title: "Buzz Potter dies; he lived, followed the life of a hobo" stretches the use of the semicolon, I'm intrigued--so much so that I must follow this life of a hobo.

What is a hobo? The definition given in my early years came from the corners of Aunt Lil's mouth, "a train hopper." Buzz Potter made a point of letting his readers know that a hobo's lifestyle is not that of a bum or tramp. Although newspapers were the best friend to homeless bums, tramps and hoboes, Potter said, "The difference between a hobo and a bum or tramp is that the hobo reads the newspaper first."

Aunt Lil tended the fueling needs of hoboes on summer noons by putting a plate of food out back on her steps for the "guys that hop trains." I distinctly remember what it was like to look into the eyes of the hoboes outback of Aunt Lil's house. The blues, greens and blacks of their deep-set pupils told me they were all very old souls, content with life as they knew it, and housing tales that would tantalize my restless feet. I wondered about Buzz. I tried to read his eyes through the obit photo but couldn't map any stories out of the faded picture. Instead I contacted Susan Langworthy, Buzz's life long soul mate in Nisswa, Minnesota and spent a few hours with her.

Before my visit with Susan, she had sent me issues of *Hobo Times*, a magazine edited and published by Buzz Potter, who went on to be president of the National Hobo Association (NHA). The *Hobo Times,* introduced in the late 80s, began as a small journal consisting of stories, poems and updates of wanderlust travels. It grew over a decade into a nationally distributed magazine with 8,000 copies printed and displayed in major newsstands.

In addition to editing and publishing the *Hobo Times*, Buzz wrote monthly columns. After reading the volumes Susan sent me, I gathered that Potter was opinionated, loud and insistent on having the last word, hence an editor. I knew after reading several pieces that if Buzz were still alive and sitting in that home on Gull Lake, I could walk right into a derailing conversation with him due to our polarized views on politics and other issues. We'd end up pissed, no doubt. Why? Because I am also opinionated, loud and content, all right, most happy having the last word.

So why would I want to write a piece on someone like this? Because in addition to those grandiose outward characteristics, inside Potter dwelled his vulnerable twin, called his conscious. This part of Buzz wrote poetry and believed in respecting the environment and promoting freedom of speech. He believed in love, in truth, in free and kindred spirits. He believed in keeping the lore of wanderlust alive and in spreading his money around like manure, fertilizing good causes, just like Dolly Levy. Because of those values, I write about this cool person. First some history…

Potter started wandering on trains at age 15, leaving when summer vacation started and returning just in time for the first day of school. "Every time I hoboed, I came back twenty years smarter," Potter said. He undoubtedly dueled with thugs while traveling the tracks, making an honest living and always moving so as to never wear out his welcome.

His rides offered him apprenticeships as a migrant harvester, rodeo helper, carnival worker, casual laborer and heavy equipment operator. Although Potter didn't start writing about his adventures until years later, he had a photographic memory that stored these years like camera reels in his mind until at his half-century point, when Potter gathered his first poems into a collection to send off to his sister, Rita. The cover letter accompanying the collection said, "The anthology, if that's what it is, is my first attempt at anything other than jingles or complex technical reports. It may also be my last. I have no inspiration at present to write any more."

In 1988, Potter published *Northern Pacific University: An Anthology of Hobo Poetry and Selected Reprints from the Hobo Times Magazine.* Potter stated in an interview, "I called it the Northern Pacific University…

It taught me to trust my own instincts and that if you honestly try to do the right thing and don't expect to get something for nothing, you'll do all right." Potter's work is very visual, and a bombardment of feelings explode onto each page in his everlasting rides across the open plains, in search for no one or nothing but the bittersweet taste of freedom.

The last route Potter took was in July, 1996, when he rode the # 15 Burlington Northern west from Minot into Whitefish, Montana. This was his first ride after many years of settling in as an entrepreneur of various businesses that included mining, guest lecturing to college geology classes, inventing 17 patents, consulting mining operations, and starting his own mortgage company. One thing about the hobo life that doesn't change is a need for diversity. Throughout his absence from actual rails, Potter continued to write about his traveling experiences, romanticizing the wanderlust that takes over the spirit of people who allow their feet to take them to unknown destinies without too much fear getting in the way.

Potter's earlier poems, a gathering of love and life written as sonnets and minstrels during his first three years with Susan, have gone unpublished. Their moods move from despair to anger to self-loathing to self-acceptance to an inner peace that gently blows forth like a lazy steam engine lullaby whistling in the distance. In one of his later poems he refers to Susan as his angel and writes, "She, in essence, helped me find that long lost garden of my mind."

Another piece about Susan was written shortly after they met at dinner at Breezy Point. The next day Susan returned to the cities to be told by her husband that he was leaving. She was devastated. Needing a friend, she contacted Potter, and three years later they shared the same view on Gull Lake. The poem, "Don't Cry My Susan," tells a story of climbing destiny's heights in order to view life panoramically. The piece ends with, "I can see the summit; we're almost there…save your tears for the summit, and if you then must cry my Susan, cry for joy, and I'll cry with you."

Susan shared the better part of her afternoon with me, answering questions that at times made her cry. She had just returned from Britt, Iowa, the site of the annual Britt hobo convention, where there was a eulogy for

Buzz. Ashes were to be scattered, but Adman forgot to bring them so remembrances were spoken at the hobo cemetery instead.

I asked Susan what she thought Buzz would want to be remembered for, and she said, "Not his business entrepreneurships; he'd rather be remembered for his poetry. I think he'd want to be remembered for that more than anything. There was talk at Britt of honoring Buzz with the title of Hobo Poet Laureate. I think Buzz would be happy about that."

I'm not a believer in much involving the afterlife, but even before Susan talked about Buzz's presence still around the house, I felt him. I think Buzz was there, listening in on most everything. Probably for Susan's protection; after all, who was this mad, loud, opinionated woman from the Twin Cities coming into her home to pry into the lives of souls deceased? Just another crazy free spirit wanting to celebrate a cool kindred spirit, that's all.

Buzz left life one March morning, staring out at the rippling waters of Gull Lake, probably after stubbing out his smoke and smiling off to the wind. Susan will host a Nisswa celebration in his honor in September. Many of the hoboes will be there eulogizing Buzz in one way or another. Adman might even bring his container of ashes to fertilize the land and waters. After all, Gull Lake is sacred hobo territory. Fiddles will be singing, and the loons on Gull Lake will be wailing right along. Susan will pass glasses of Nightrain and although I'll pass the booze by, I'll toast Buzz in my heart, remembering what Buzz once said, "Once a hobo, always a hobo." I'll leave saying what Buzz was known to close with, "Happy rails 2-U." May he rest in peace.

> *And we'll all meet again with these wayfaring men,*
> *By the river on God's peaceful shore.*
> *There'll be coffee and stew and dry firewood too,*
> *And at peace, we will wander no more.*

---Buzz Potter, excerpt from "The Hobo Cemetery"

New Brighton resident Suzanne Nielsen, grew up in St. Paul and teaches writing at Metropolitan State University. She enjoys writing poety, fiction and memoir.

Depression Years on our Northern Minnesota Farm
by Anastasia "Stacy" Vellas

Mama was always the first one up. She'd dress quickly and hurry over to the cold heater. I could hear her from my bed across the room as she put chips and logs on the coals left from the night before in the big barrel heater. When the chips lit she opened the damper and fire and smoke would roar up the stovepipe. The fire crackled and spit from the snow still on the logs, and the roar usually woke my sisters sleeping next to me.

After lighting the heater, she'd hurry on to the other end of the house to the big wood range, open the little door on the front, and put in kindling. On top of the kindling she'd place the wood Connie and I had split and carried in the night before. She'd lift the lid and set it to the side while she lit the fire from the top of the stove. Soon pleasant odors came drifting back to us in our beds.

One by one each of us would get up and dress around the warm heater while Mama made breakfast. Outside the wind howled as it whipped across Third Guide Lake and up the hill passing our house.

"It must be 40 below zero," Daddy would say as he dressed and held his hands to the heater's warmth. "Someday, someday we're going to California, where it's warm all year."

While Mama cooked breakfast on the range over the wood fire, the oven and the water reservoir next to the oven were heating up. The stovepipe that passed between the two warming ovens kept food warm until it was served. Each warming oven had a narrow lift-up door. After breakfast, Mama let the fire die down until lunch unless she planned to bake bread.

Mama always fixed a good breakfast. She felt that everyone needed a good breakfast to start the day. For herself, she felt eating was just a necessary chore. "Breakfast is ready," she would say from the kitchen end of the one-room house, as she bustled around getting everything on the table. She seldom sat down. If she did, she sat next to the stove ready to jump up and get anything we needed.

Sometimes Mama made bread pudding for breakfast. She mixed cocoa, eggs and sugar in a big bowl. Then she poured hot milk over it until it was all melted together and added her teaspoon of vanilla (real vanilla, she always said). She gathered up the stale slices of bread and crumbled them in until the cocoa mixture was all absorbed. Then she baked it in the oven until it was dry. While the pudding was baking she'd skim off fresh cream from the top of a wide mouth gallon jar of milk and whip it by hand with a rotary beater until it stood in high, smooth white mounds. Dishing out a bowl of chocolate bread pudding, she'd hand us each a big bowl. I poured some milk around the pudding and passed the pitcher on to Connie. Then Mama would top it with a big scoop of the fluffy whipped cream. It was delicious. No one ever made bread pudding like Mama.

We had 160 acres to explore, and we were always hungry. Mama made homemade bread twice a week, and with our oatmeal she'd give us a slice of bread and butter. Sometimes she asked Connie and me to help churn the butter, for it was a tedious task. She'd get out the two-gallon glass churn she had ordered from Montgomery Ward in St. Paul. Taking the cream skimmed off the top of the milk that had been saved in the cellar for several days, she'd pour in enough cream to fill the glass churn about half full. Then Connie and I took turns turning the handle. As we turned the handle, the gears fastened to the lid turned paddles around and around inside the jar splashing cream against the sides. Then we could not see what was happening on the inside. It seemed to take forever, and we'd wonder when the butter would come. About the time we were ready to give up, all at once butter began forming around the paddles, and soon big globs were clinging to the paddles making it harder and harder to turn.

"Mama, Mama, the butter's ready," we would shout. She would come and take over, turning the last few turns of the handle until the butter was nice and firm. When it was the right texture she'd drain the fluid into a pitcher. Reaching into the churn she would remove the butter by handfuls and place it in a bowl on the table next the churn. Then she washed the churn. As soon as the butter was firm, she would cut each of us a slice of homemade bread and spread it with the fresh homemade butter. It was so good.

Mama thought Guernsey cows gave richer milk so she always kept a Guernsey. Sometime in the fall, Daddy would lead the cow away to the neighbor's, and in a day or two he would go get her and lead her back home. The next spring there would be a little calf in the stall with Bossy. Mama said the first milk was for the calf because its colostrum was good for the calf. Sometimes she would milk out some of the colostrum, mix it with sugar, flour, and vanilla and make us a delicious pudding.

After three days she began milking the cow again twice a day. The calf nursed often all day. Milking the cow was important, she told me. "You always sit on the right side of the cow. And you speak to the cow so you do not startle her, or she might kick you. Set the stool back a little. Put the pail against the stool, lock it in place firmly between your knees and slant the pail so the milk goes in. If the cow should kick the pail, the stool will protect it, and your knees will keep it from tipping over. And BE SURE you strip the cow until there is no more milk, or she may go dry."

Connie and I both learned to milk, and we enjoyed the task. Sometimes we would set up our sisters, brothers and a cat or two and squirt milk in their mouths. When the cow had a lot of milk sometimes it became very tiring. Then we were not so sure we wanted to milk her again. It was always Mama's chore.

Daddy took care of the bees. All winter long the hives stayed in the warm barn so they wouldn't freeze. The bees lived off the honey they had made the summer before from clover and crab apple blossoms, the wild-flowers and garden. In spring, when the frost was past, Daddy would get out his bee hat with the wide brim and cheesecloth that covered his face and shoulders. Then he would put on his gloves and bring out the bees, box by box, and place them near the crab apple trees on the hill. If one stung him, he'd say, "That son-o-ba-gunna"

He removed each tray and carefully extracted honey leaving a small amount for the bees to live on until they began making more honey. Mama heated it in a large kettle. When it was hot and thin she strained it through several layers of cheesecloth. She put the hot honey in mason jars with a layer of melted beeswax on top, and she gave us kids each a wad of bees-wax to chew. We always had honey until Daddy stopped keeping bees.

We always had plenty of food. Mama canned vegetables, and Daddy hunted deer, ducks and rabbit.   We raised chickens for eggs and to eat. Mama went out to the chicken coop, grabbed a nice fat chicken by its head and swung it around and around until she broke its neck. Then she let it go, and it flopped on the ground until it died. When it stopped flopping she took it to the house, put it in a pail of hot water to loosen the feathers. Then she pulled out the feathers and saved the small soft ones to make pillows or a feather bed. Nothing was wasted except the head and feet. You couldn't give those to the dog because the dog would start killing chickens. Once a dog started killing chickens you had to destroy the dog.

We raised strawberries to can and to sell. In the fall we picked wild blueberries from the patch on the hill south of Third Guide Lake, and Mama canned them. Sometimes in season we picked cranberries in the big bogs over by Charley Hansen's place along the east side of Hidden Lake for Mama to can for the next winter. I remember picking wild gooseberries along our road and eating them on the way home from school. In the fall the bushes along the road had hazel nuts. Some were single and some were double. They were smaller than filberts and tasted wonderful. We even liked the chokecherries that made your mouth pucker.

Though times were tough, these are wonderful memories. During the Depression everyone was dirt poor in Minnesota. But I guess, in most ways, we were really much richer than we are today.

The Vellas family home near Swatara

The Old Swatara School
by Anastasia "Stacy" Vellas

The Swatara School was the center of my social life. Before I started school, my only friends were my brother, my sister and my cousins. We lived back in the woods and seldom went to town, but in 1933 at the Swatara School I met my best friend, Marcella Wilcowski, and we remained friends throughout our school days. A few hundred adults lived in the Swatara district, and each had five to eight children who attended the big school on the hill. Everything is built on a hill in Minnesota, as spring floods can wipe out a town in a few minutes.

We were fairly isolated on our farm seven miles from town, especially during winter when snow was knee deep and the lake was frozen. We were three quarters of a mile from the main road on my Grandfather's homestead that he staked 1901. The snowplow kept the main road cleared, but the snow on our country road was over two feet deep, and we had no plowing equipment. During winter Daddy could not get the car out to the main road, so whatever we needed from the store in town I had to bring home on the school bus.

Of course, we needed very few things. Our cellar had storage shelves stocked with quart jars of homegrown beans, corn, peas and strawberries we children had helped pick and Mama had canned. Sacks of potatoes, rutabagas and cabbages lined the opposite side of the cellar. We also stored canned blueberries from the patch on the hill. Sometimes bears would be there across the berry patch eating berries while we picked our share.

Daddy was a hunter from necessity. We always had venison, fresh in winter and canned in the summer. We were told from an early age never to tell that Daddy shot a deer or the game warden would come and take Daddy to jail. So when Daddy would load his gun, sling it over his shoulder and take off into the woods, we knew in the morning we'd have to go and help carry the meat home. And that was a tough job for a kid.

Sometimes other kids would come to school and say, "My dad got a deer last night." I'd say, "You aren't supposed to tell!"

Daddy was also a seasonal trapper. He would set out maybe 40 traps, line them up and mark the trail so he could find them. I learned to skin minks, muskrats and weasels (ermine) used to make fine furs coats for rich ladies in the cities. My brother Connie and I trapped weasels.

Daddy raised strawberries and sold them. In 1937 he made a deal with Montgomery Wards to fill their orders for young strawberry plants. Early each spring we would dig up young plants, count them in bunches of twelve, and tie them with string. Daddy would fill orders and ship them directly to the buyers, and he began to make more money. When the strawberries ripened, we would pick and pack them in quart boxes. Daddy would drive to the nearby towns of Remer and Walker west of Swatara, and my brother and I would go door to door and ask people if they would like a box for ten cents. This was very humiliating for me, but my dad came from Greece, where peddling was an honorable profession. Strawberry and fur sales comprised our income for several years.

Just before school began, Mama would get out the new calico ordered from Montgomery Wards, wash all the flour sacks and make us new school clothes. She'd sit down at her old Singer sewing machine, and the treadle rocked back and forth as the needle flew up and down the seams. Soon there were brand new dresses for us girls and shirts for my brother. The flour sacks she had washed and saved were turned into nice crisp underwear. They were kind of rough at first, but after a few washings with lye soap, the cloth began to soften up.

Mama sent away for ready-made snowsuits, coats and shoes. One year she ordered our shoes from Sears Roebuck. When I tried on my shoes, they were too small, but they were so pretty, and I didn't want to send them back. I told Mama they fit just right. That was the worst decision I ever made, because my feet hurt all winter. The tight shoes curled my last three toes back under, and I still have a problem

My brother Connie, my sister Rose and I had 160 acres, a boat and all summer to explore, but when the crops were in and the canning finished, it was time to go back to school. Then everything changed. The farther north you go, the shorter the days are in winter. Winter mornings, we would be dressed before daylight.

Mama fixed hot breakfast of steaming oatmeal or farina with rich milk from Bossy, our Guernsey. From the warming oven she would take out hot buns and spread them with thick homemade strawberry jam. Our school lunches were either peanut butter or jelly sandwiches in a tight lard pail.

I was 5 when I entered first grade in 1933. I was told to walk to the mailbox and catch the bus. I walked three quarters of a mile to the main road every day by myself. No one asked, "Can you do it? Are you Scared? Do you want me to go with you?"

I don't remember being scared. I had roamed the local woods and walked to the main road for over two years. Seldom did we see other people except when we went to town so I was very shy. When winter came, I had to ski to the main road, hide my skis in the woods, and get on the bus. When the bus brought me back, I would find my skis and ski on home. I could ski home in less than half the time it took to walk. Once it was so cold waiting for the bus my toes were frostbitten before I got to school. It was very painful, and I was crying. My teacher took off my socks and shoes and soaked my feet in cold water until they stopped hurting.

When I was in third grade, before my brother started school, there was a porcupine that waited in the road by the big rock every day when I came home from school. I would throw rocks and yell at him, but he would just look at me. I had to wait until he decided to cross the road and go off into the woods in his own good time before I dared go on home. I was terrified. I couldn't go around him. My parents had warned us that porcupine quills would go in real deep, and our dog Pal had come home with quills, and I had seen Daddy pull them out with pliers while Pal whined and pawed at his nose.

We were the last to get on the bus next to the Cass County Line. I'd get in and sit with Marcella Wilcowski, and we would visit. Her farm was about three miles down the road from us on McKinney Lake. Sometimes we walked to each others' houses to play. Marcella's family planted a garden, and her dad worked all year on the WPA crew, which meant they had more money. He made $30 a month so they could afford to buy real butter. Sometimes Marcella brought butter sandwiches for lunch, and I'd exchange one of my jelly sides for one of her butter sides, and we'd each have a butter and jelly sandwich. Betty Cook was an only child, and she had a banana for lunch every day. I envied her and said, "When I grow up I'm going to buy all the bananas I can eat." And I did.

Since my parents were snowed in, I was expected to walk down the hill to Trepanier's Store in Swatara, buy groceries and bring them home on the bus. We only needed a few things, like sugar, lard, or peanut butter. On shopping days I quickly ate my lunch, put on my coat, and walked to Trepanier's. I gave George Trepanier the list at the front counter, and he walked around the store picking up the groceries we needed, and he charged them to the Vellas account. When he finished gathering groceries and was adding up our bill, I said, "I'd like that piece of penny candy."

Knowing how tight my dad was with money, George would ask, "Did your dad say you could buy candy?" I knew it was wrong, but I looked him right in the eye and lied, "Yes, Daddy said if I brought home the groceries I could have a penny candy." I must have been convincing, because he slid back the glass doors and reached into the big case below the cash register and handed the candy to me across the counter. Returning to school I walked slowly up the hill savoring each lick, each bite, and I never did get caught.

The Swatara School was a monument to our small town in northern Minnesota. Built for $80,000 in 1921, it stood as a beacon on the hill overlooking Swatara. In winter the building was warm from radiators generated by the big wood furnace in the basement. On the east side of the school were four-foot lengths of cordwood stacked in long rows.

A long hall with shiny hardwood floors led to huge doors that opened into classrooms on the east side. The auditorium was on the west side. There were stairs on each end of the hall, and best of all, in the bathroom were two sinks to wash your hands, toilets that flushed, and soft paper-- a big change from our outhouse on the farm.

Christmas was always a special time at the Swatara School. Each child had a costume and a part in the Christmas play. There was candy and lots of good things to eat. I especially loved the German cookies Mrs. Gressons made. One Christmas the principal sent the bus out to pick up the snowed-in kids and their parents. My mother bundled us all up, and our whole family went to the Christmas play, and the bus ride was wonderful. The bus was warm, Mama brought quilts to put around us, and we snuggled together. Every time the bus stopped the lights went on, and my parents greeted other families that got on. We sat near the front, and I could see the headlights on the snow-covered roads. Piled on the side of the road were huge drifts the snowplow had made for the bus to get through.

Our teachers were well-respected in the community. We were under their care while we were away from home, and we obeyed them because it was expected. Most of us were backwoods kids and very shy. I would never have done anything to make my teacher angry with me, and I don't remember any teacher ever being cross.

Our teachers were young and pretty, and they were always smiling and happy but serious. One of my teachers taught me to tap dance, which I'll do anywhere, anytime, if I'm asked. Another teacher taught me the Minnesota State Song, and I have yet to find a fellow Minnesotan to sing it with me! But I try. Anywhere I see a vehicle with a Minnesota license I ask them to sing the state song with me, and give them a copy.

When I was 10, one of my teachers had us memorize poems. Then she said we could write our own poem and recite it to the class. Well, I liked that idea, but as hard as I tried I couldn't write a poem. So I asked my aunt, Elsie Berg to write one for me. I proudly read it to the class as my own, but I never felt right about that plagiarism. Because of my love for poetry (and partly out of guilt), I began writing my own poems and have continued writing poetry ever since.

I loved recess. I would run out to be first to the swings. Swinging higher and higher I would look down on the roofs of houses along the street just below the school grounds and recite Robert Lewis Stevenson's poem..

"How do you like to go up in the swing...up in the air so blue,
Oh I do think it's the pleasantest thing ever a child could do" ....and end
'Til I look down on the grass so green...Down on the roofs so brown.
Up in the air I go flying again...Up in the air and down."

As I looked down on the roofs from my swing on the hill, I'd thrill just to be alone with my poem. And when I became a teacher I stood in the door of my classroom watching kids who had learned the poem swing while the rest in the class were still memorizing.

The year I was 11, the school began a hot lunch program. Two cooks would cook all morning, and delicious aromas drifted up while we studied. At noon we picked up our lunch pails and went to the cafeteria. The ladies brought us each a big steaming bowl of soup, and we'd eat our sandwiches with hot soup. My dad brought in cabbages and rutabagas from our cellar to pay for our share.

The winter I was 12, I got up one morning, pulled my long stockings over my underwear that came down to my ankles, and slipped on my coat over my slip before I dressed because it was so cold. After breakfast, I put on my overshoes and walked to the bus stop. When I got to school and went to the cloakroom and took off my coat, I looked down to find I was dressed only in my slip. I had forgotten to put on my dress! I had to wear my coat all day, and even though it was 30 degrees below zero outside, it was the hottest day I ever spent at school. After that I made sure to put on my dress before breakfast.

When I was 13, our teachers Mr. Knapp and Miss Kenny got married. They were wonderful people and we loved them dearly. Some people in town decided to give them a shivaree, and Connie and I were among the kids invited to go along. We walked along the railroad track for about a mile to their house, banging pans with sticks. The shivaree was a gathering at the house of newlyweds by friends who made noise until the couple let them in and gave them hot cocoa or cake and coffee. We made so much noise that Joe and Sarah heard us coming and ran out and hid in the barn. We knocked and knocked on their door, but no one answered. Then we started looking around outside. Finally, Connie discovered them hiding in the haymow. According to tradition they had to treat us, so they walked us back to town and bought each of us an ice cream cone at the store.

The last day of school was always exciting. Parents brought in huge bowls of salad, roasts, chicken or something from their gardens. Some brought cakes or pies, all homemade and simply delicious. We would line up and fill our plates and feast with our friends. Parents visited while teachers took the kids outside and participated in games and races. By the end of the day, after saying our good-byes for the summer, we were tired and ready to go home. This was the last time we would see most of our friends until fall because people only drove to town when necessary.

The Swatara School was so strong. Built of brick and stone, I knew it would last forever on the hill overlooking the town. How I loved that old school. The town, which held dances and meetings there, was also proud of that beautiful school.

In the spring of 1993, my sister Rose and I decided to return to our hometown after 50 years and visit our old home. I bought a tent trailer, and Rose and I set out in early June. We camped at my cousin's place in Grand Rapids and set out for Swatara in my 4x4 Toyota truck. The main road from Highway 169 into Swatara is paved now, but the country roads including Old Highway 35, the road passing the school, are still gravel.

Rain started falling as we pulled into Swatara and drove up the hill from Trepanier's Store and stopped across the road from the school. We just sat there in awe, gazing at our old school in all its splendor. It was just as it was when we left for California the winter of '44. We drank in the site so awed with its splendor.

"Could we go in?" Rose asked me, "Do you think they'd let us?"

"Of course, we can; it's a public school. They can only tell us to leave," I told her. Just then, one of the doors at the back swung out, then back. We couldn't believe our eyes. We were shocked silent. We just looked at each other, saddened. The school was deserted! We sat there for awhile, not believing what we saw.

Then I drove up the hill and parked near the back entrance, and we got out. As we approached the building we saw the back door hung by one bent hinge, and the glass was broken. Part of the frame had come loose. We stepped over broken glass to enter the downstairs hall.

It was still raining as we entered the building. In the hall the hardwood floors were buckling from rain that came through broken windows. In the room that had been the library, the shelves were tipped over, and all the books were gone. As we climbed the stairs to the upper room, I ran my hand along the beautiful hardwood banisters, still as beautiful as they had been 50 years ago. Upstairs where I went to 6th, 7th and 8th grades, old school books, left behind, lay on the floor getting wet from the rain.

Outside the swings were gone, and unmowed grass grew where the playground used to be. Everything around the building from the street to the place where the bus barn used to be was covered with tall grass. It was deathly still. As I walked back to my truck I noticed the sign over the back door that still said, "Consolidated School." But the school, that once had been the center of my life, was now left to the elements. All that is left are my memories. I wrote this poem with my unshed tears.

The Old Swatara School

Brick and stone, it stands alone
Where once I learned the golden rule.
Now waving grass and broken glass
Mark the end of Swatara School.

Its broken panes let in the rains,
And wind whips down the hall...
The swings are gone, I once played on,
But the chimney stands straight and tall.

For the years gone by I want to cry
As I walk through each empty room,
But tears won't heal the loss I feel
At the plight of Swatara School.

Anastasia "Stacy" Vellas moved to California in 1944, where she worked as a field worker, a waitress, and mother to five wonderful sons. She became a teacher in 1973, and she now lives in Brawley, California.

208

The 50 stories in *Minnesota Memories 4* took place in these towns.

Hallock

Boundary Waters Area
Virginia

Swatara
Aitkin
Nisswa

Vergas
Fergus Falls
Alexandria   Foreston   Beroun

Morris

Stillwater
Minneapolis St Paul
M'tonka Mills Eagan Hastings
Echo   Northfield
Redwood Falls   Owatonna
Hardwick   Blue Earth Waseca
Sveadahl   Mn Lake   Spring Valley   Winona
Lismore   Huntley
Hollandale Waltham
Adrian Jackson   Albert Lea, Austin

Was there a story from your town in this book? Do you have a favorite true story you'd like to share with the world in *Minnesota Memories 5*? Send stories (and photos) to Minnesota Memories, 439 Lakeview Blvd, Albert Lea, MN 56007, or email them to MinnMemory@aol.com. To book a Minnesota Memories program at your library, historical society, organization, store or school, use the addresses above or call 507-377-1255.

Back page special! If you made it all the way to the last paragraph of the last page, you deserve a break. Order any book from the Minnesota Memories series for $12. For a complete 4-book set, send $46 (check, money order, or cash). Postage and tax are included.